Everything About Abstract Circles

Adult Coloring Book Vol.1

About The Artist

I grew up in an artistic family and have been an artist ever since I was a little girl.

At 17 years old I had my first professional art gallery exhibit. Later, I studied Architecture and Interior design, with my specialty being furniture and lighting design.

Over the years I have created hundreds of paintings and designed many products, such as, dog toys and clothes, furniture and a skin care/cosmetic line.

"I believe art transforms our emotions and opens our visual awareness".

Bereniche Aguiar

Art and Shop Website: www.berenicheaguiar.com

Recommendations

I recommend only using colored pencils to prevent any color bleed through on the pages. I also suggest putting a piece of cardboard underneath the page being colored, for more support, if it is desired to press hard with the colored pencils.

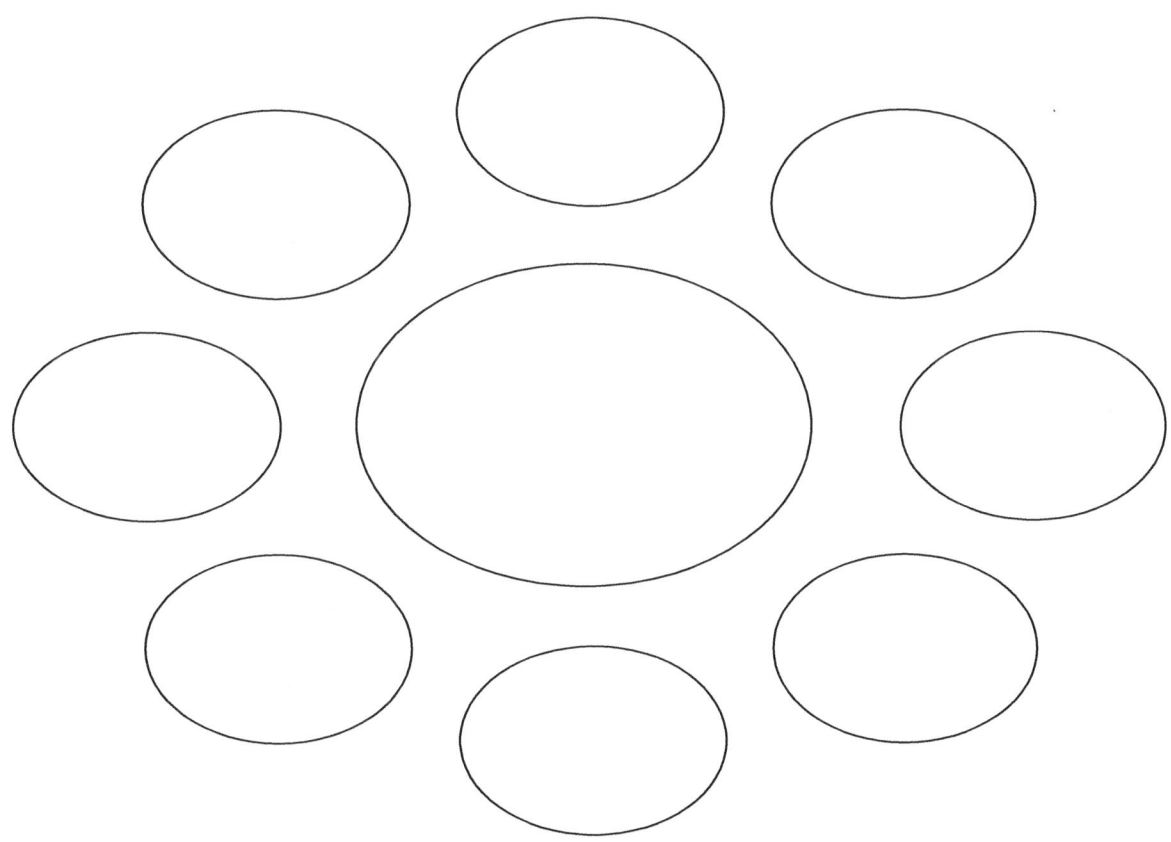

All abstract designs derived from these nine original circles.

D# 1690

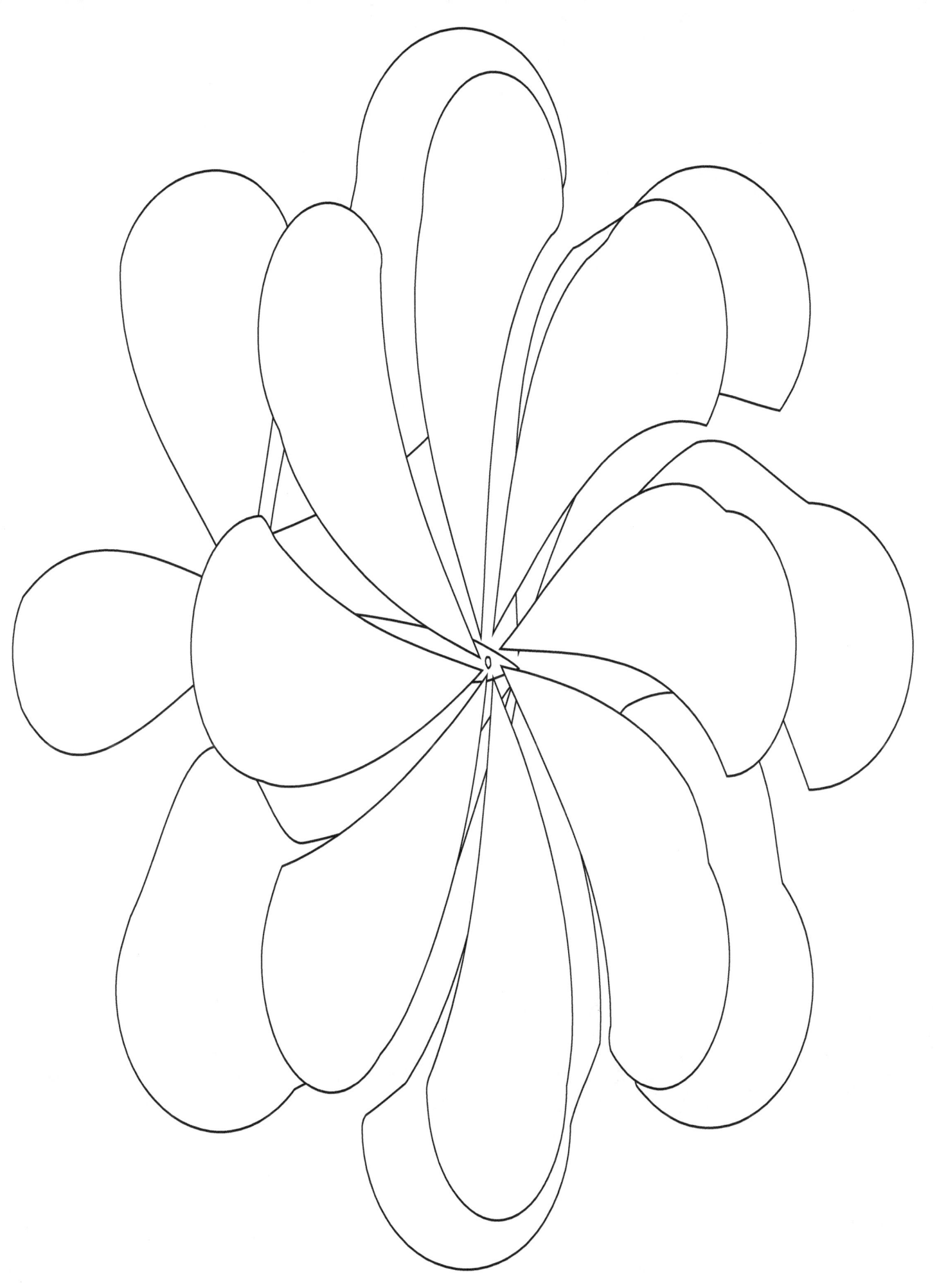

D# 1699

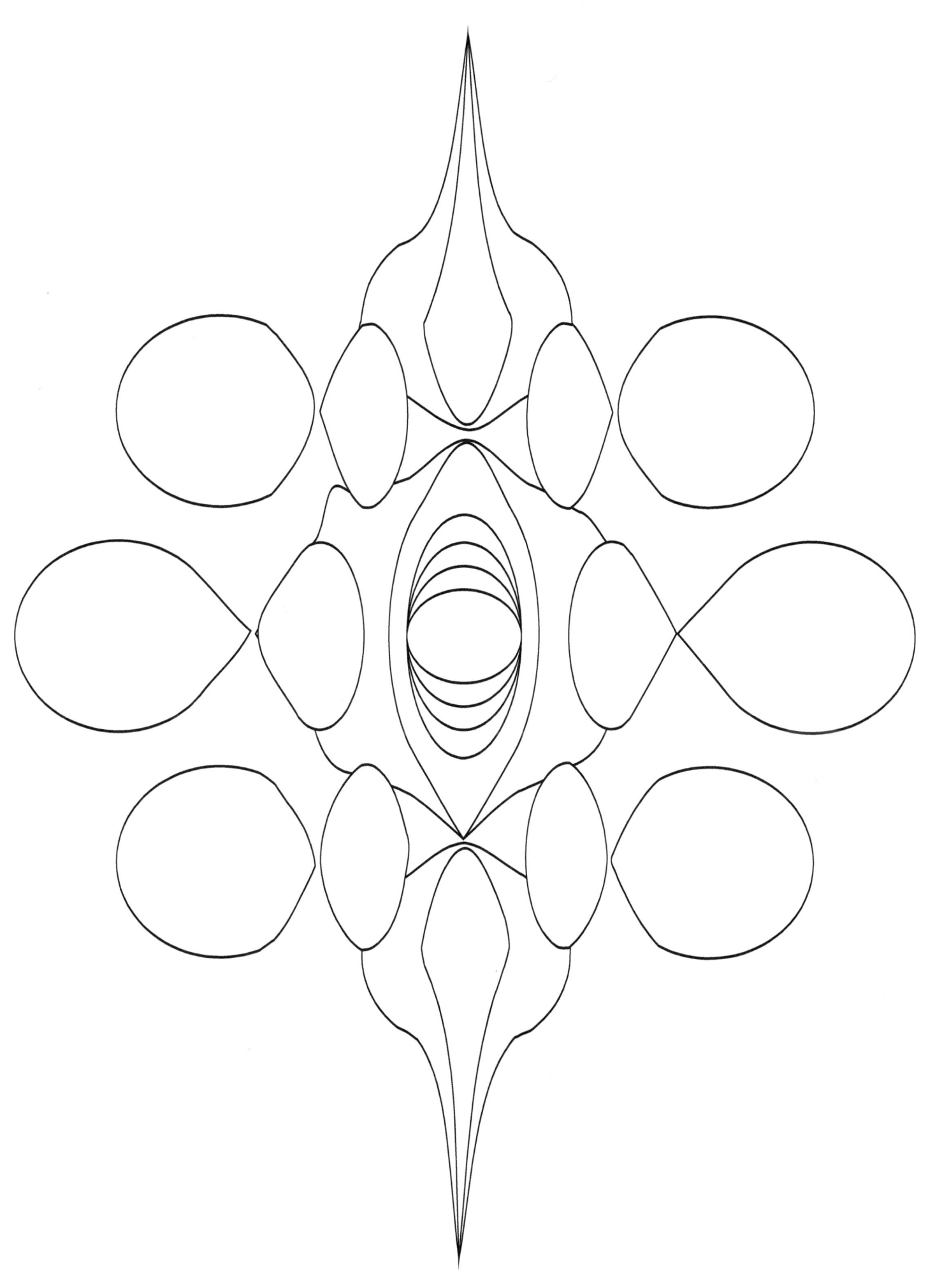

D# 1687

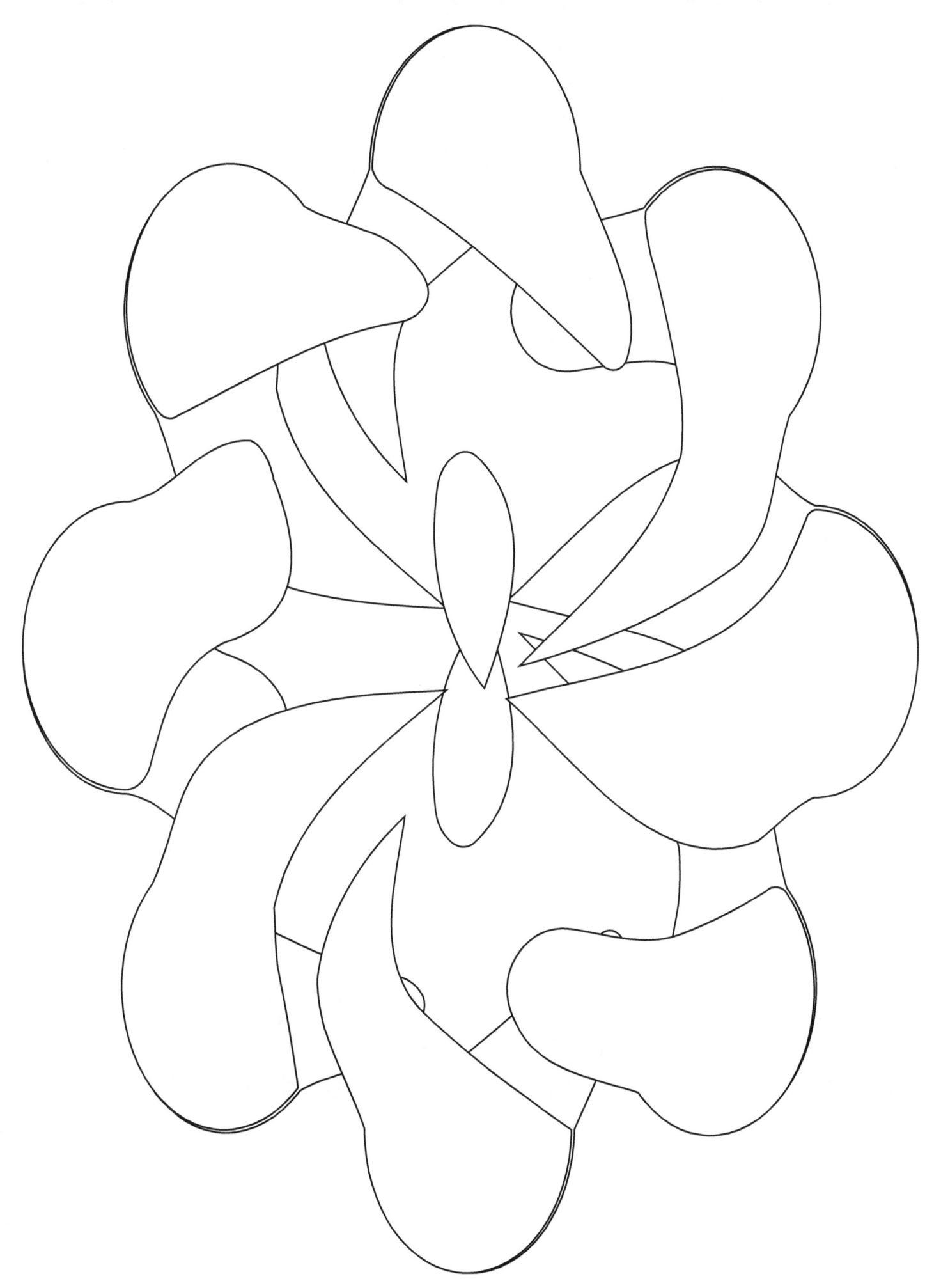

D# 1747

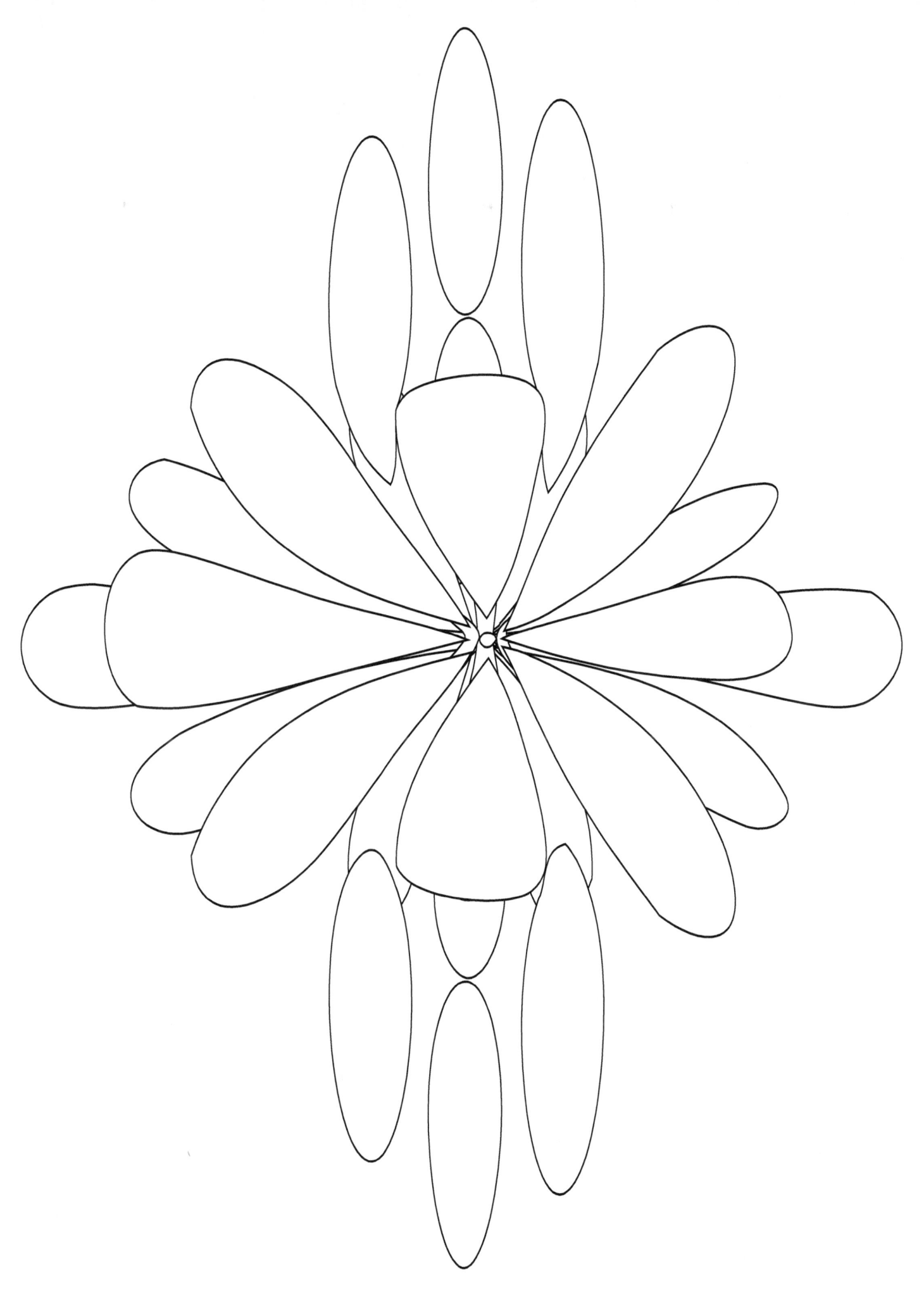

D# 1726

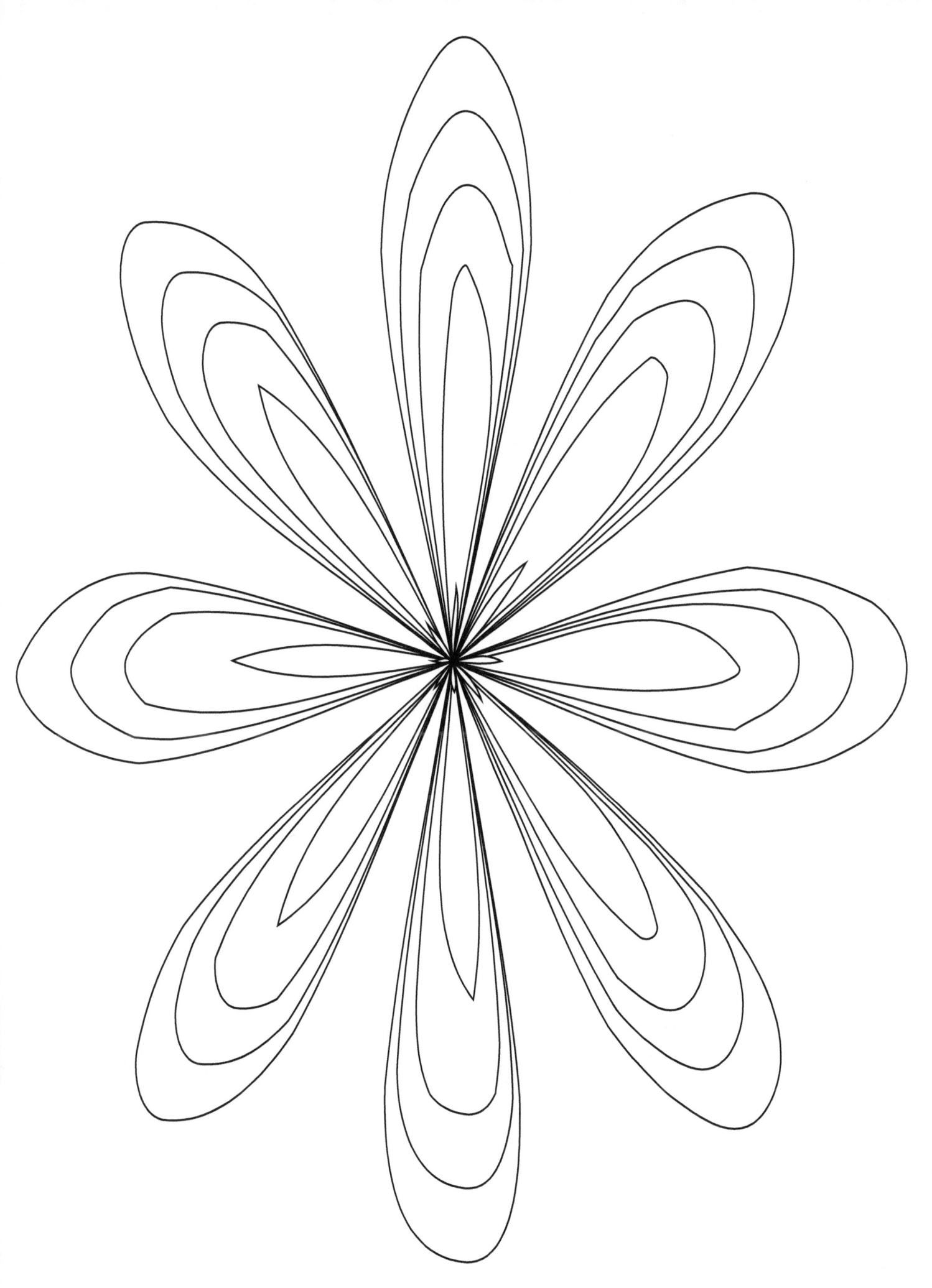

D# 1736

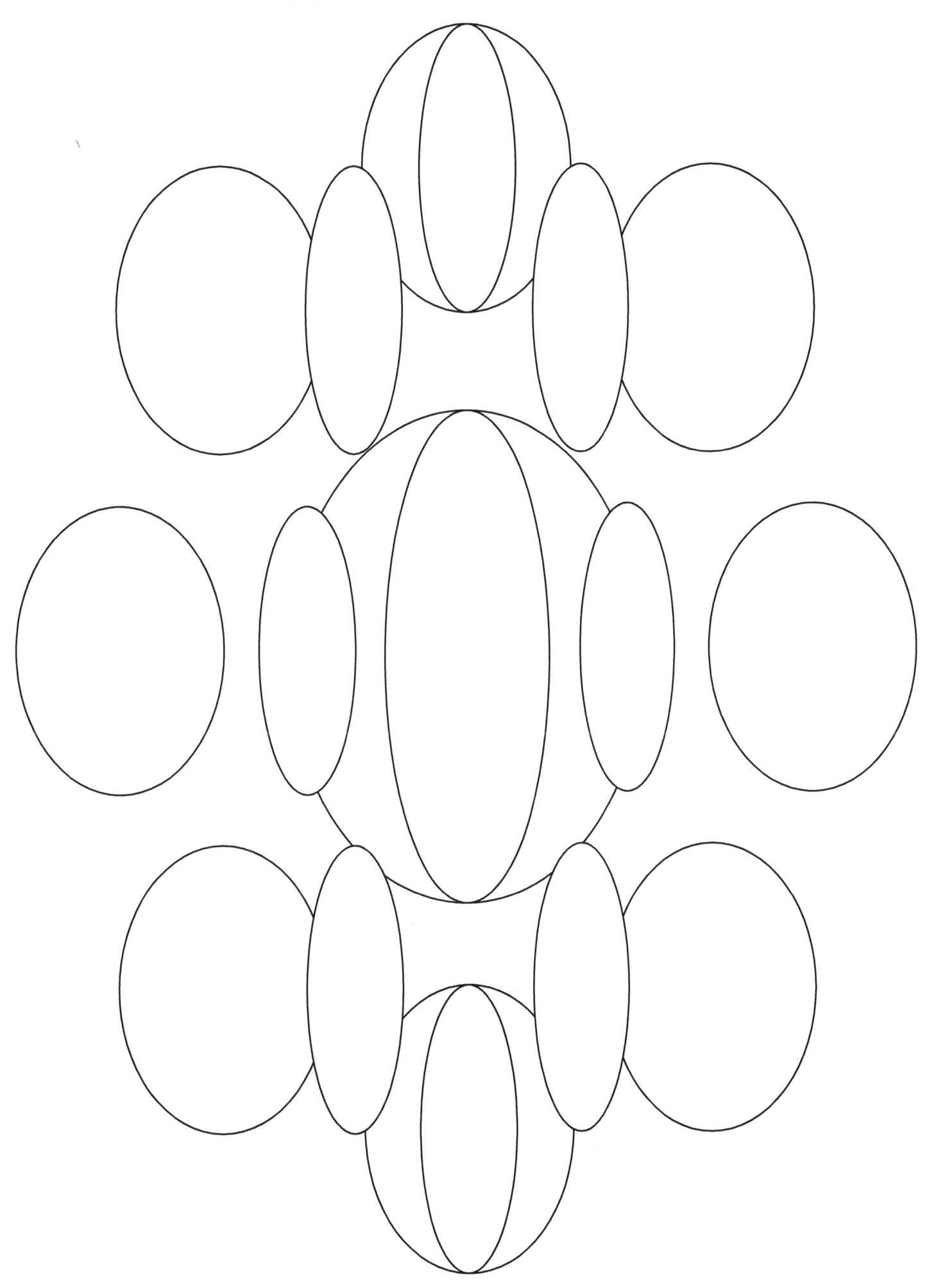

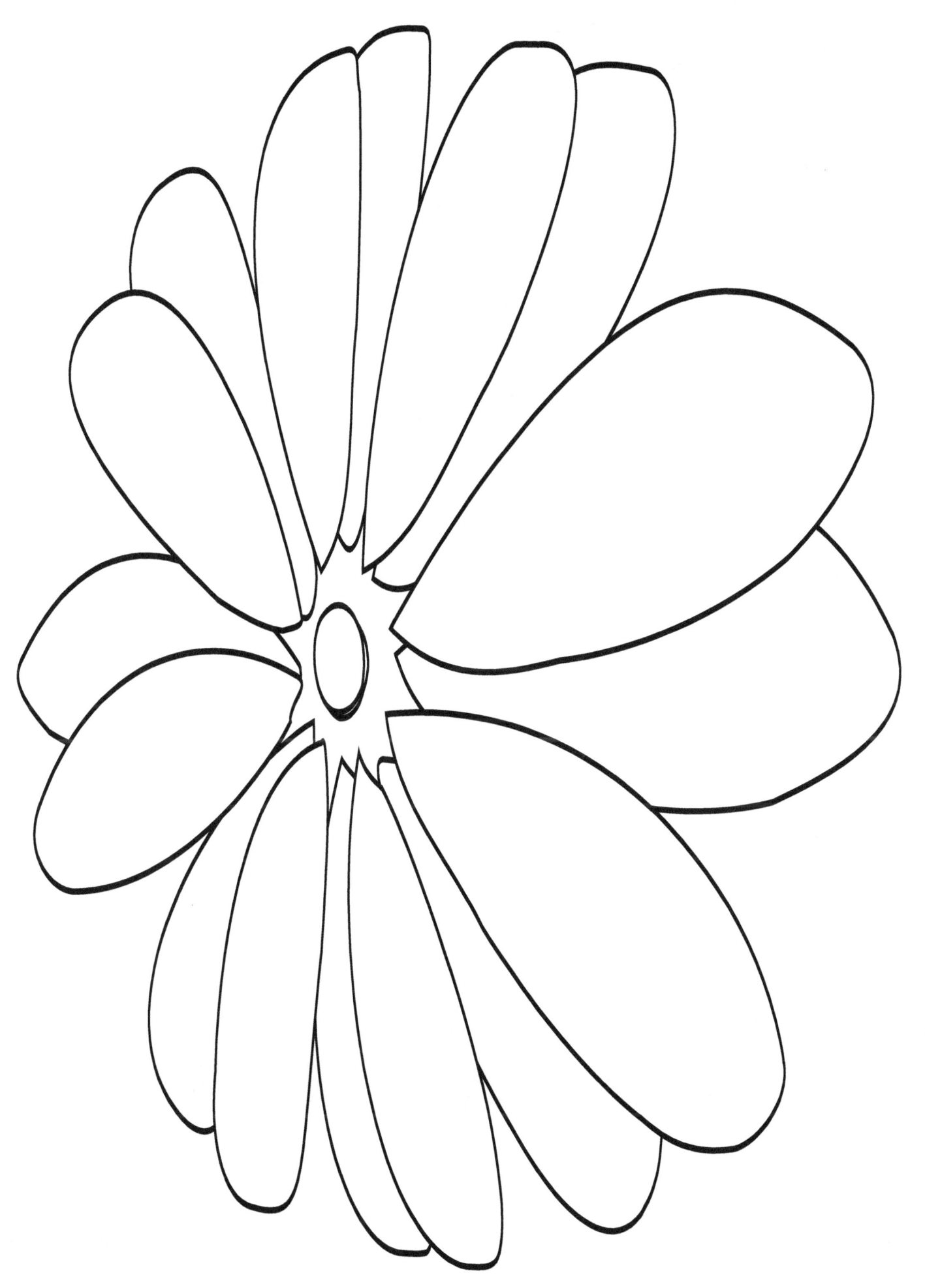

D# 1805

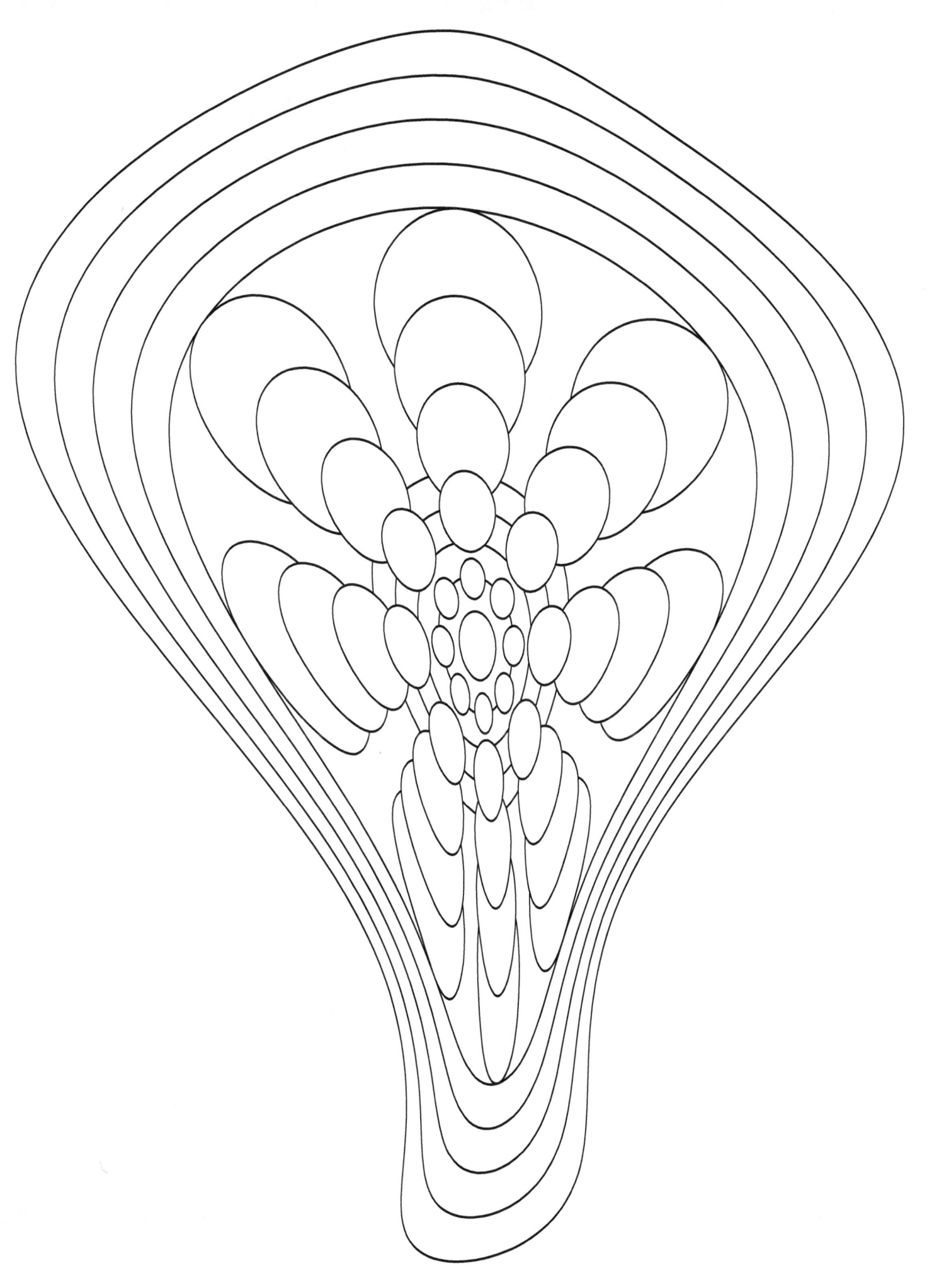

D# 1836

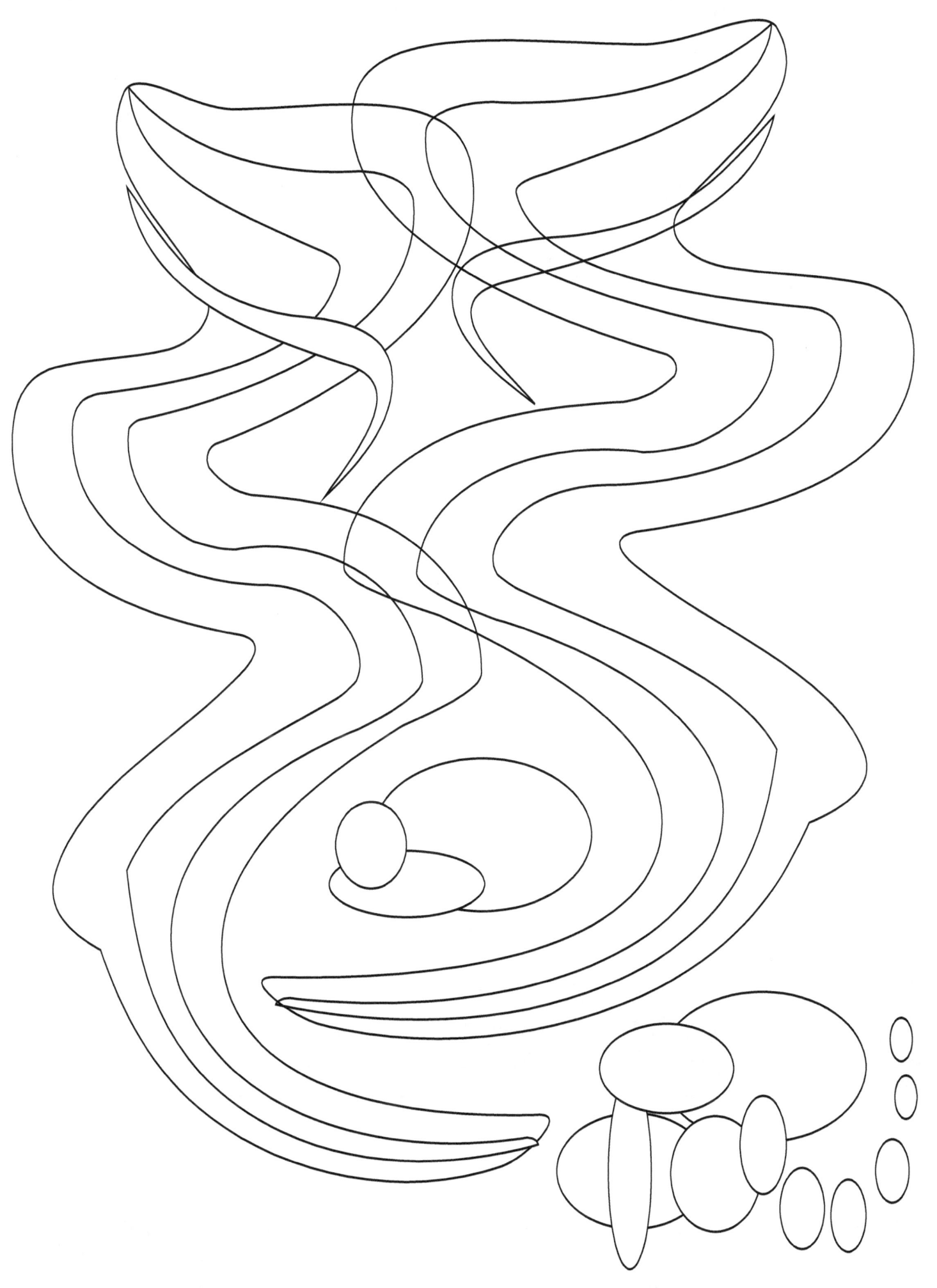

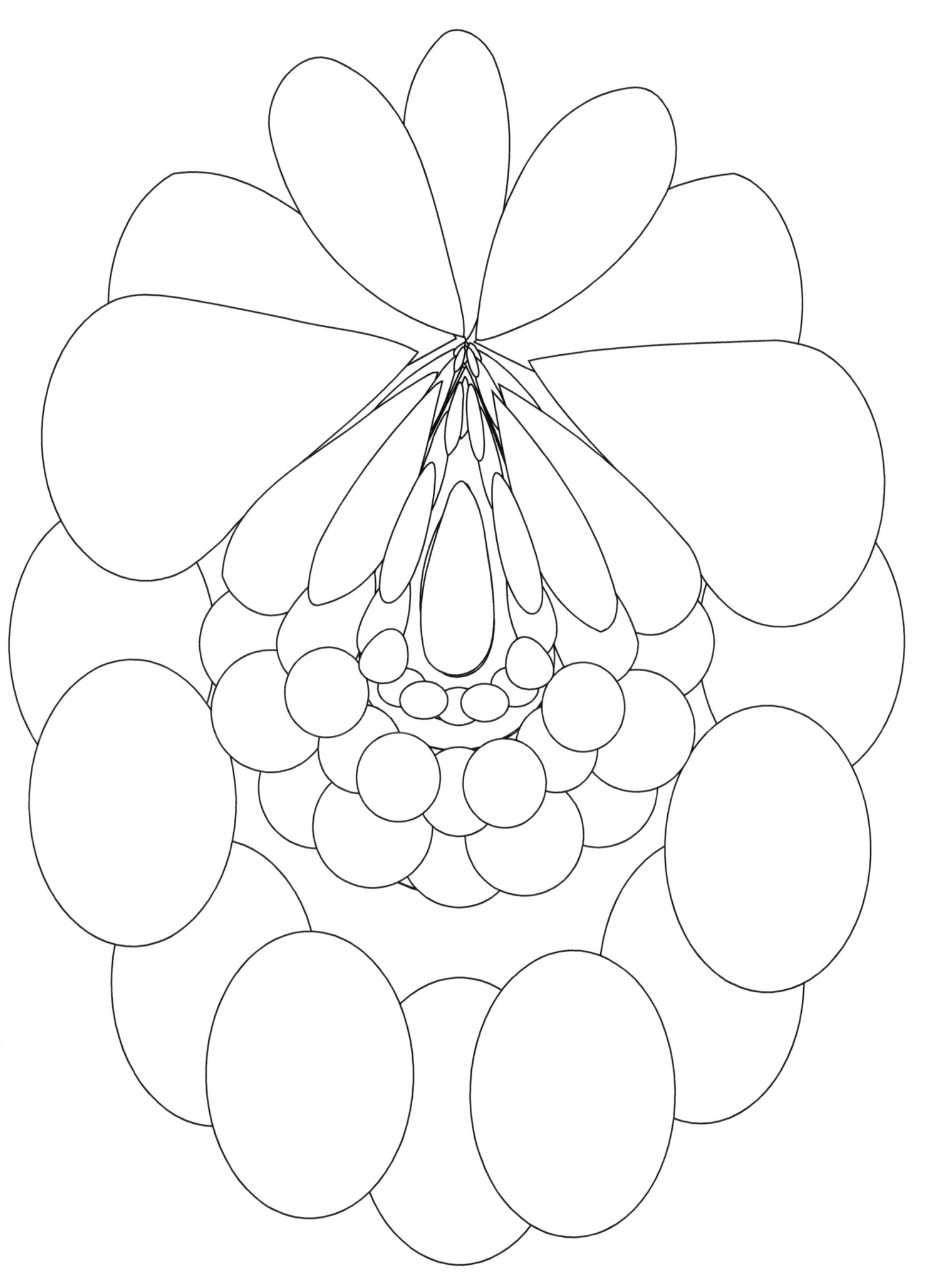

D# 1742

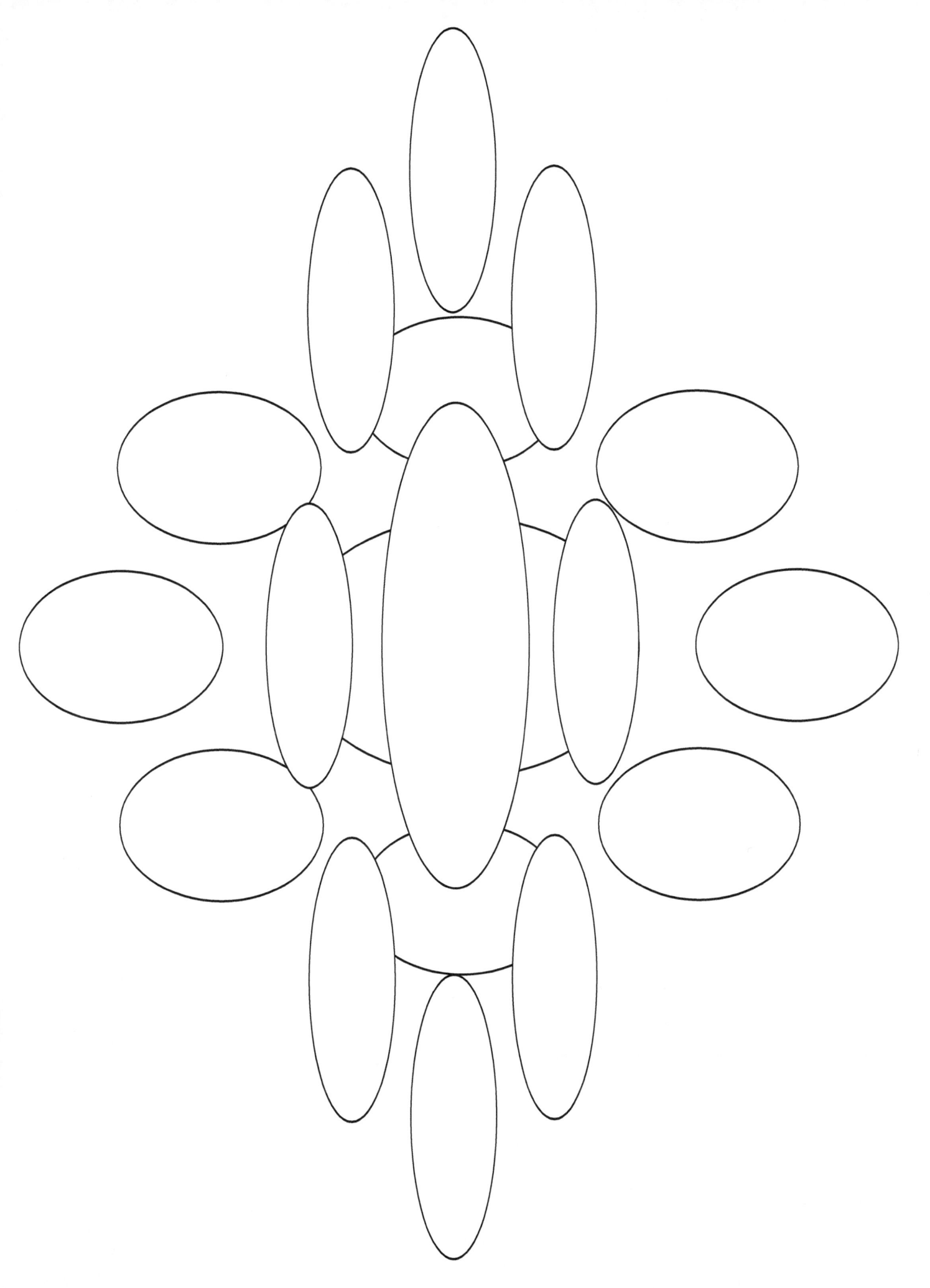

D# 1765

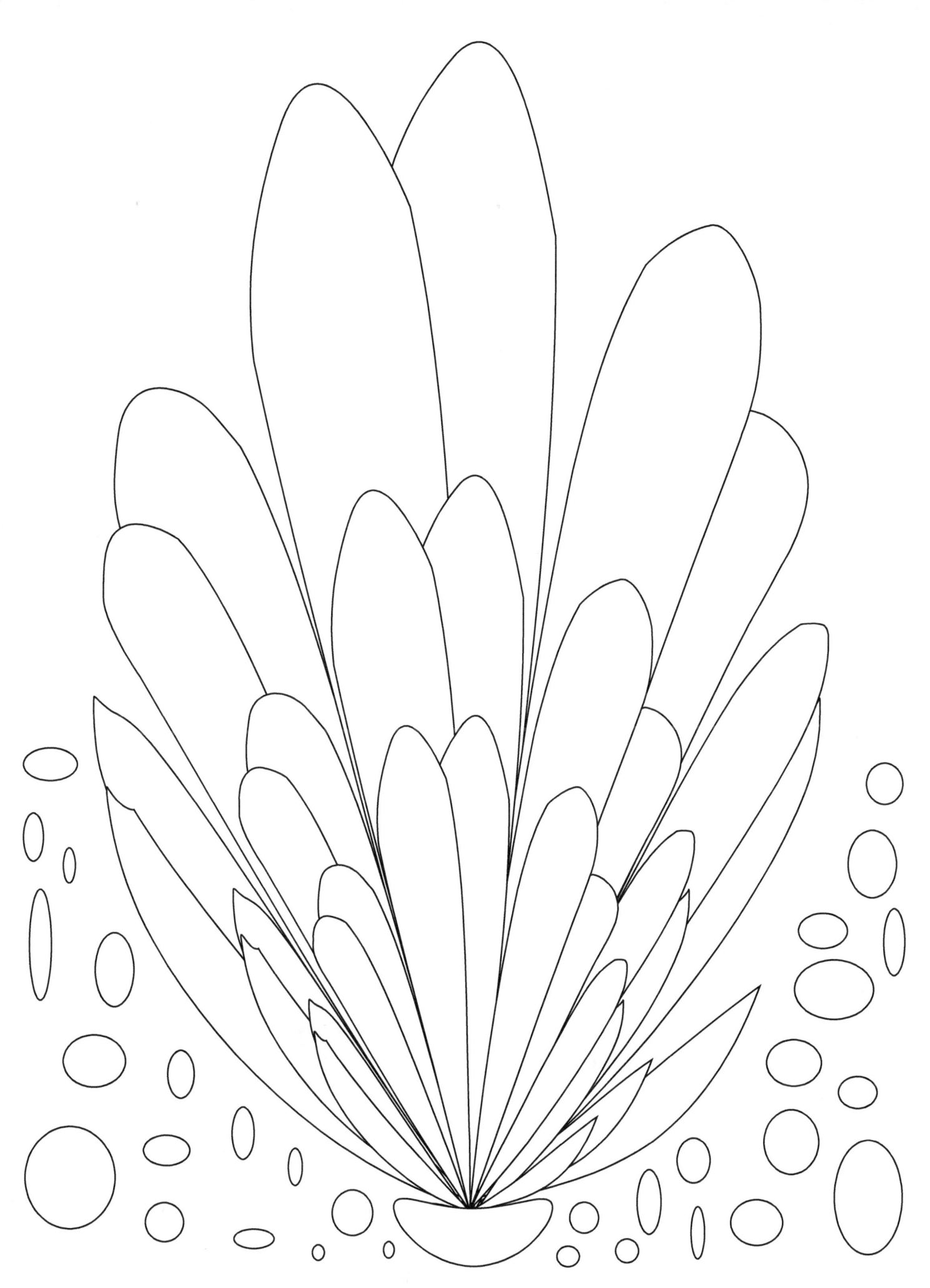

D# 1828

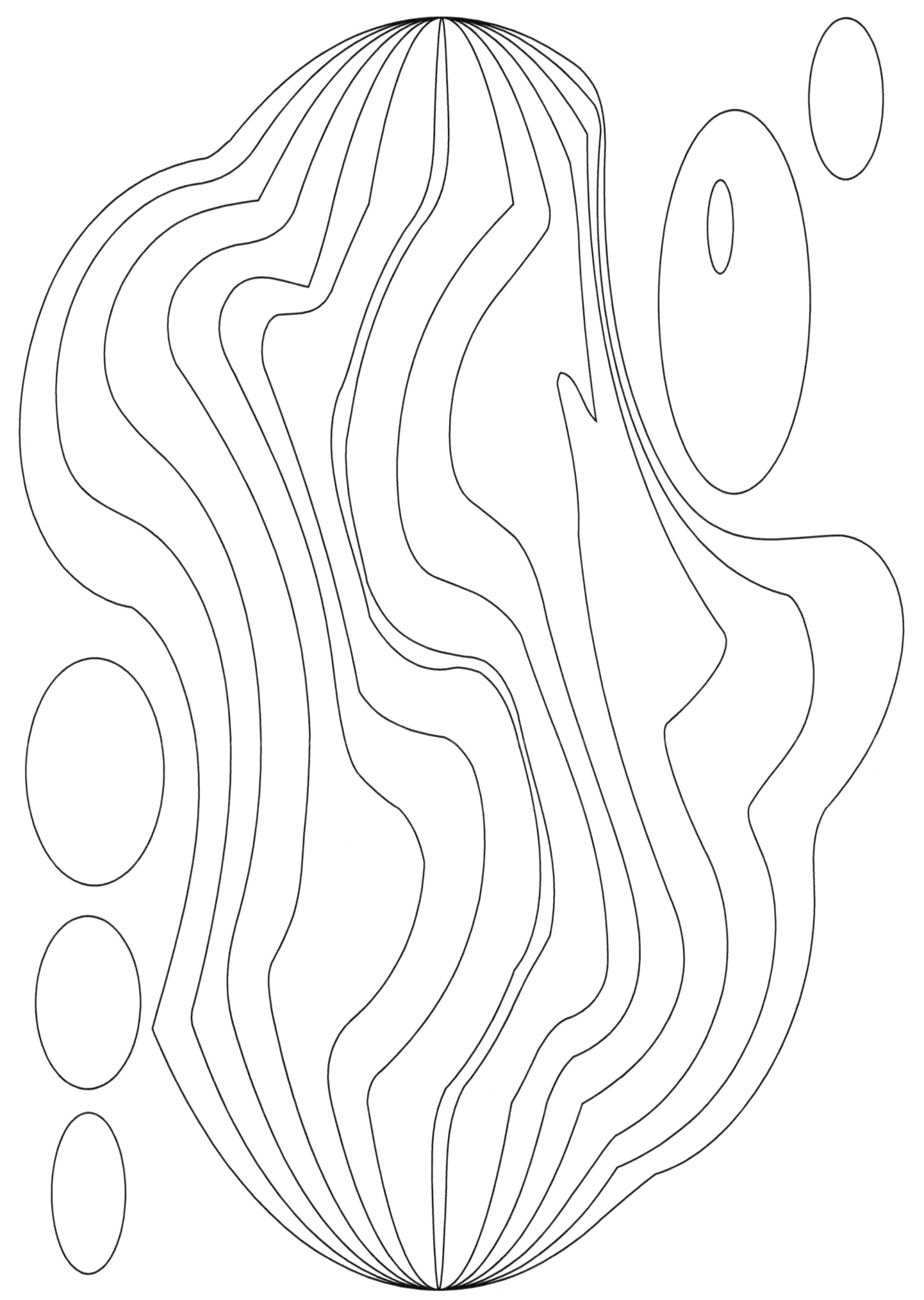

D# 1720

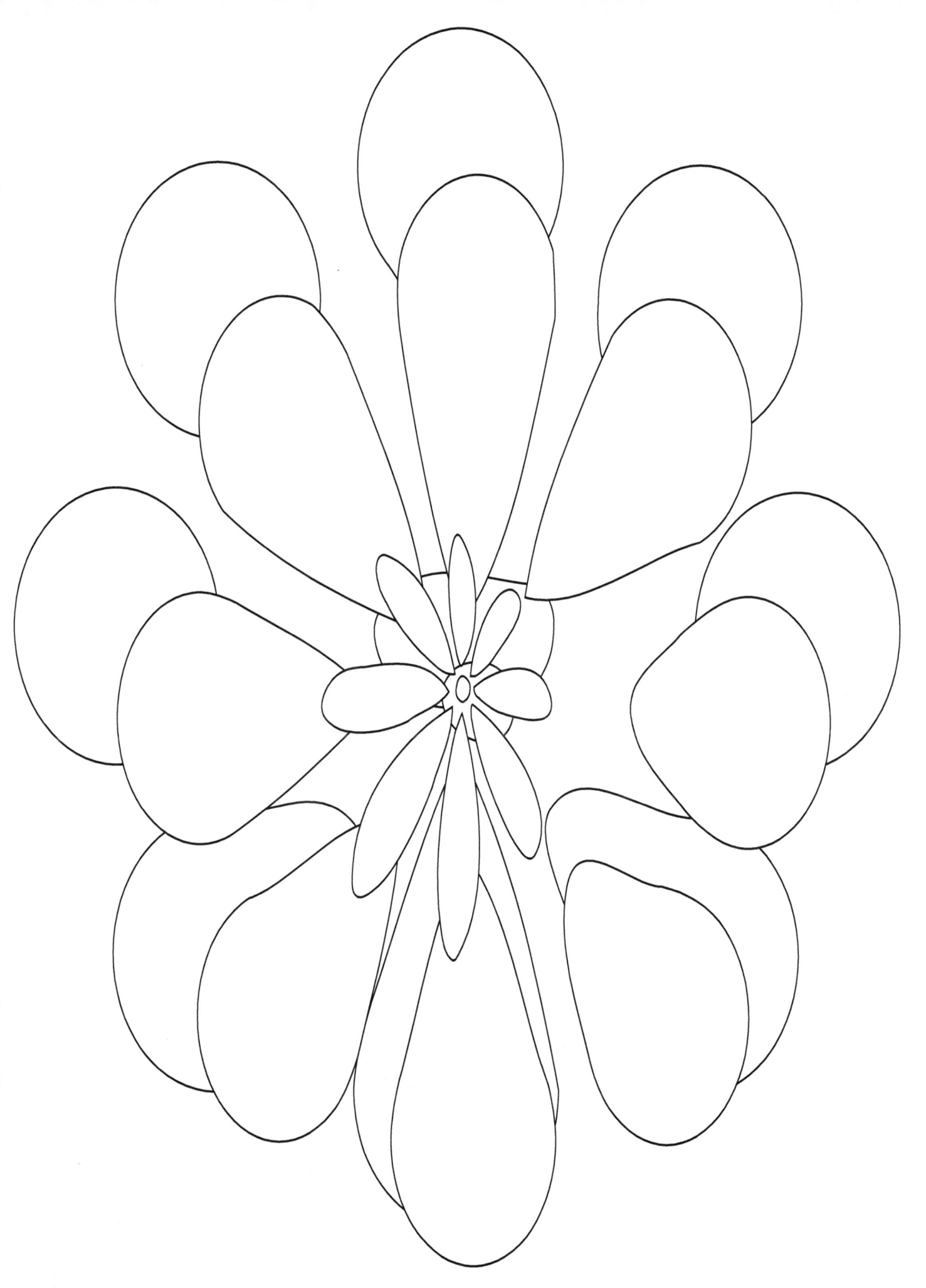

D# 1701

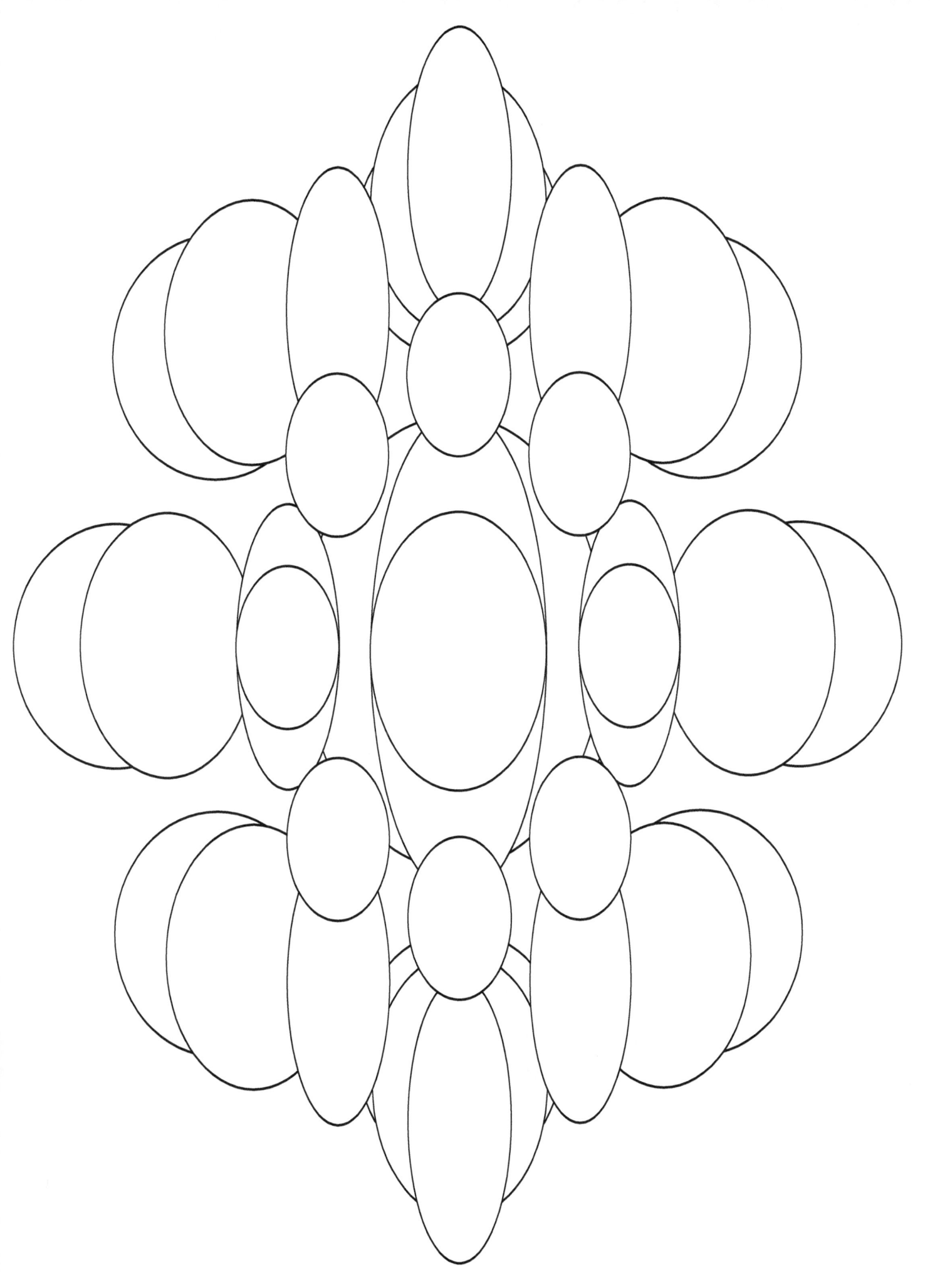

D# 1716

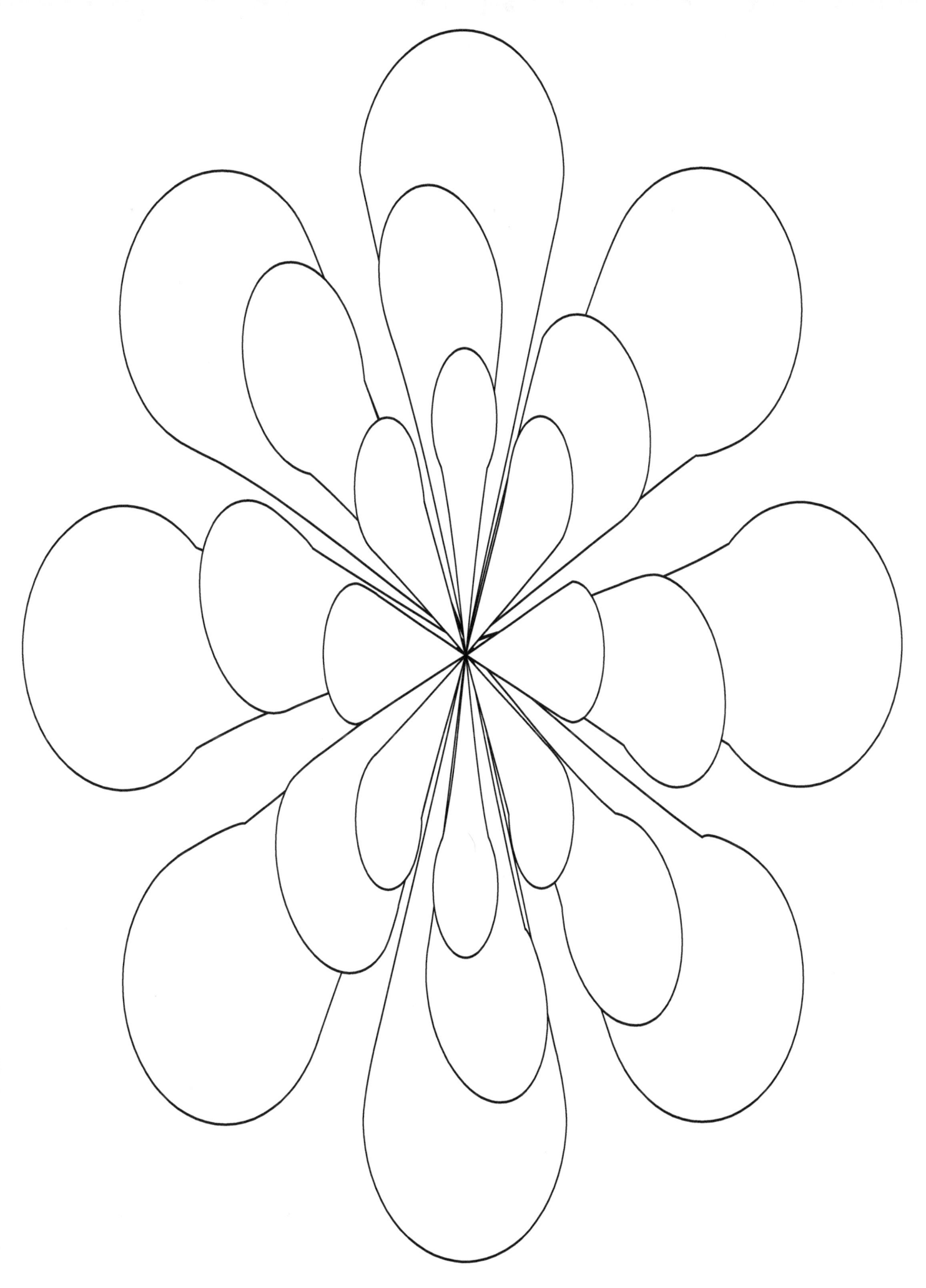

D# 1724

D# 1825

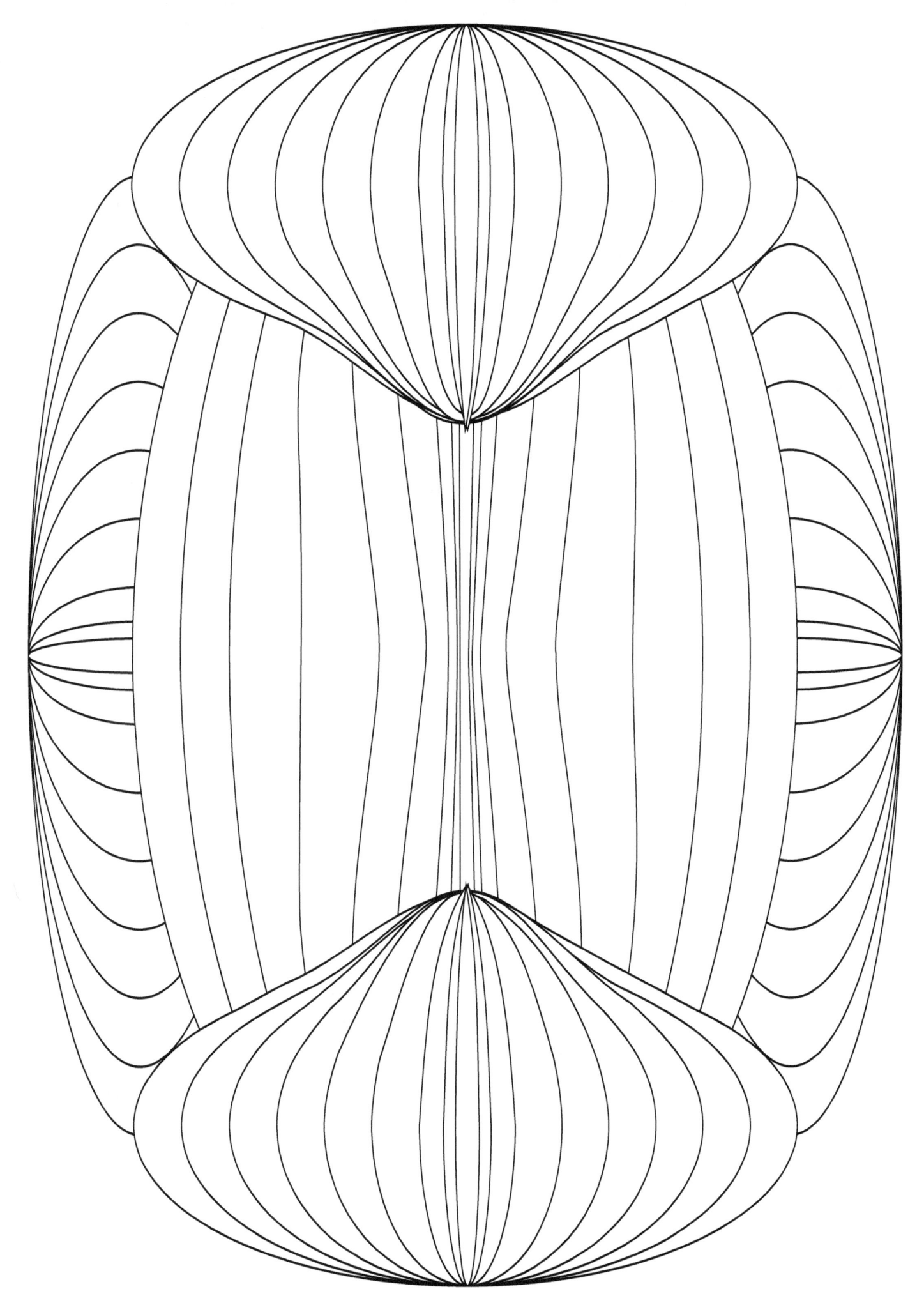

D# 1695

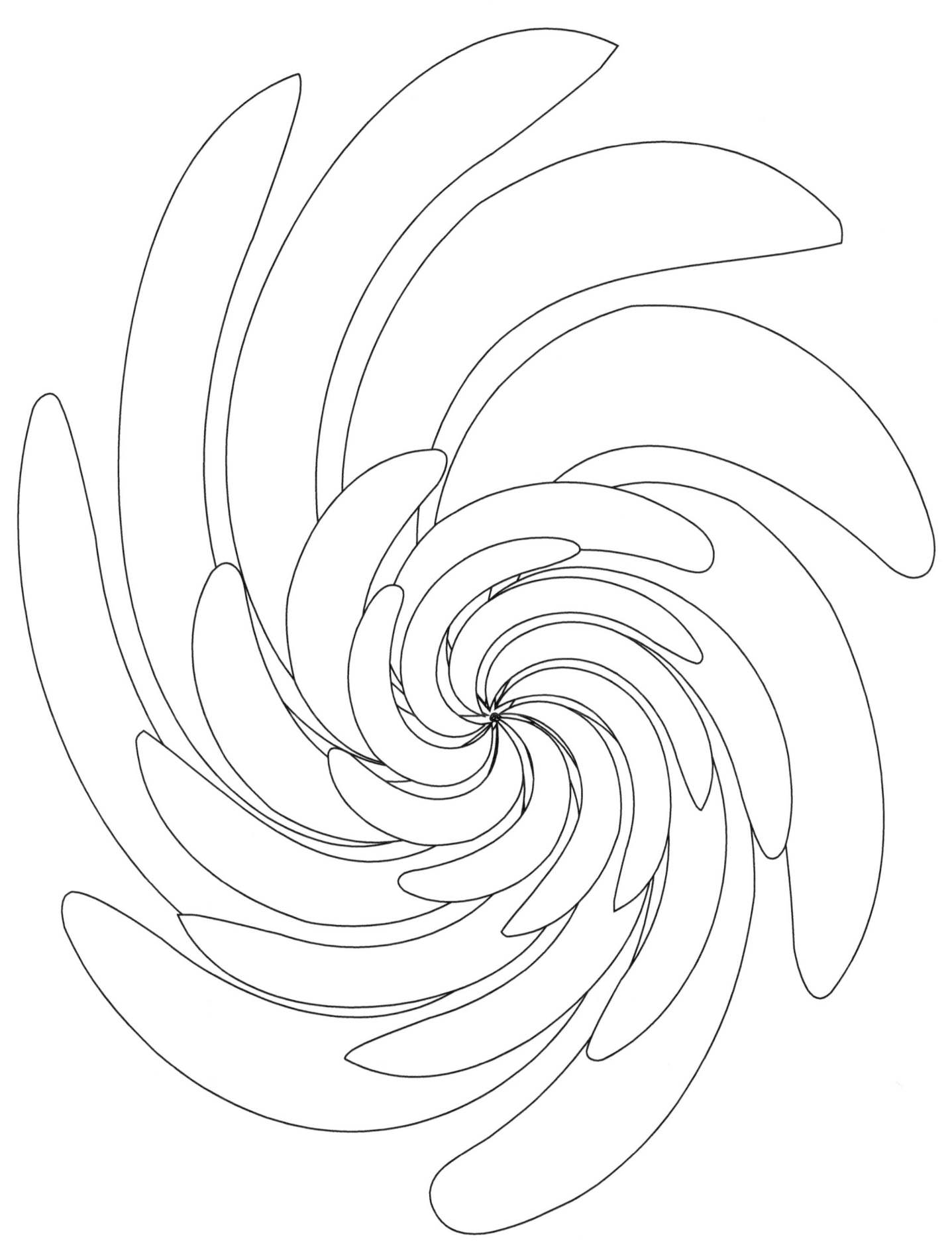

D# 1727

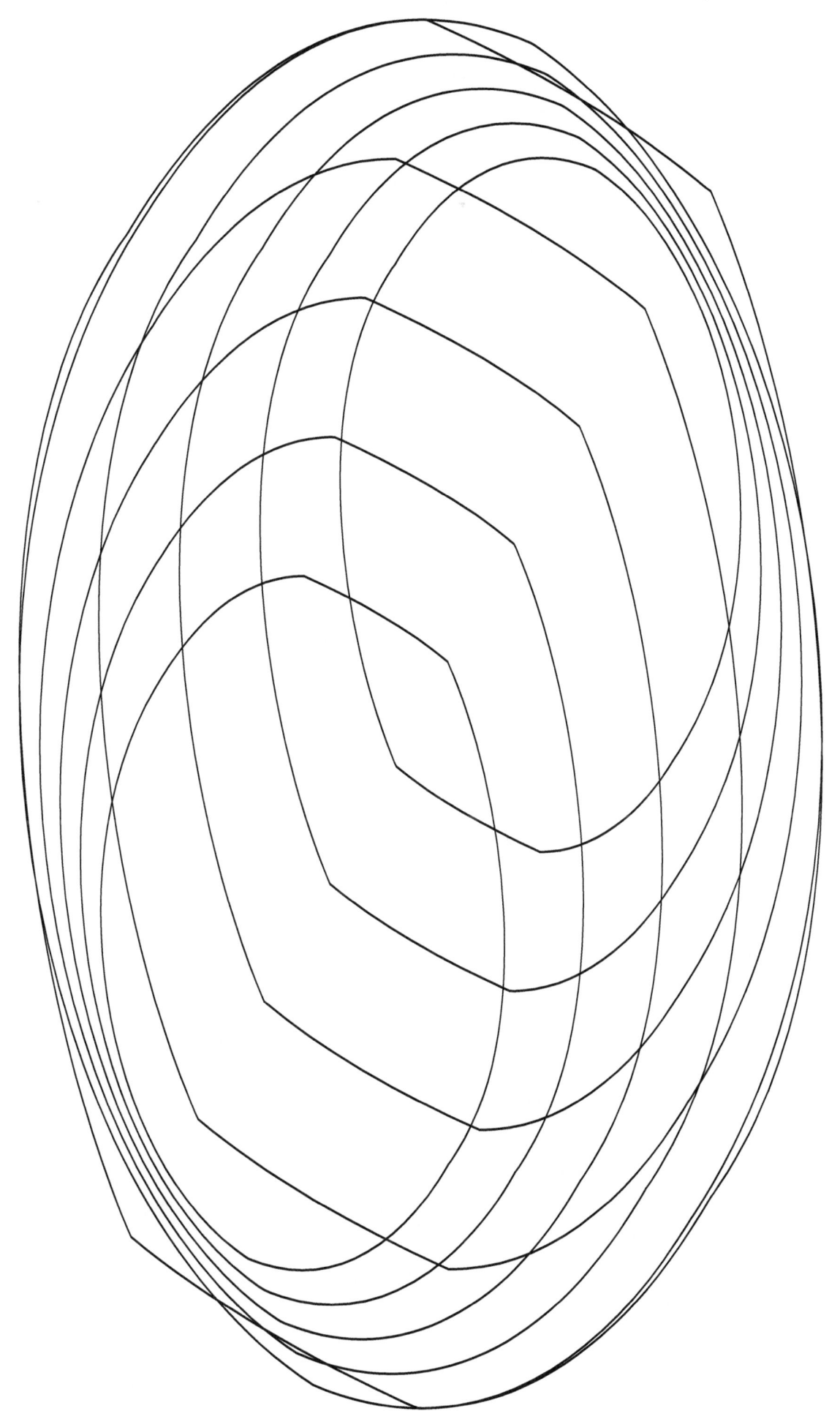

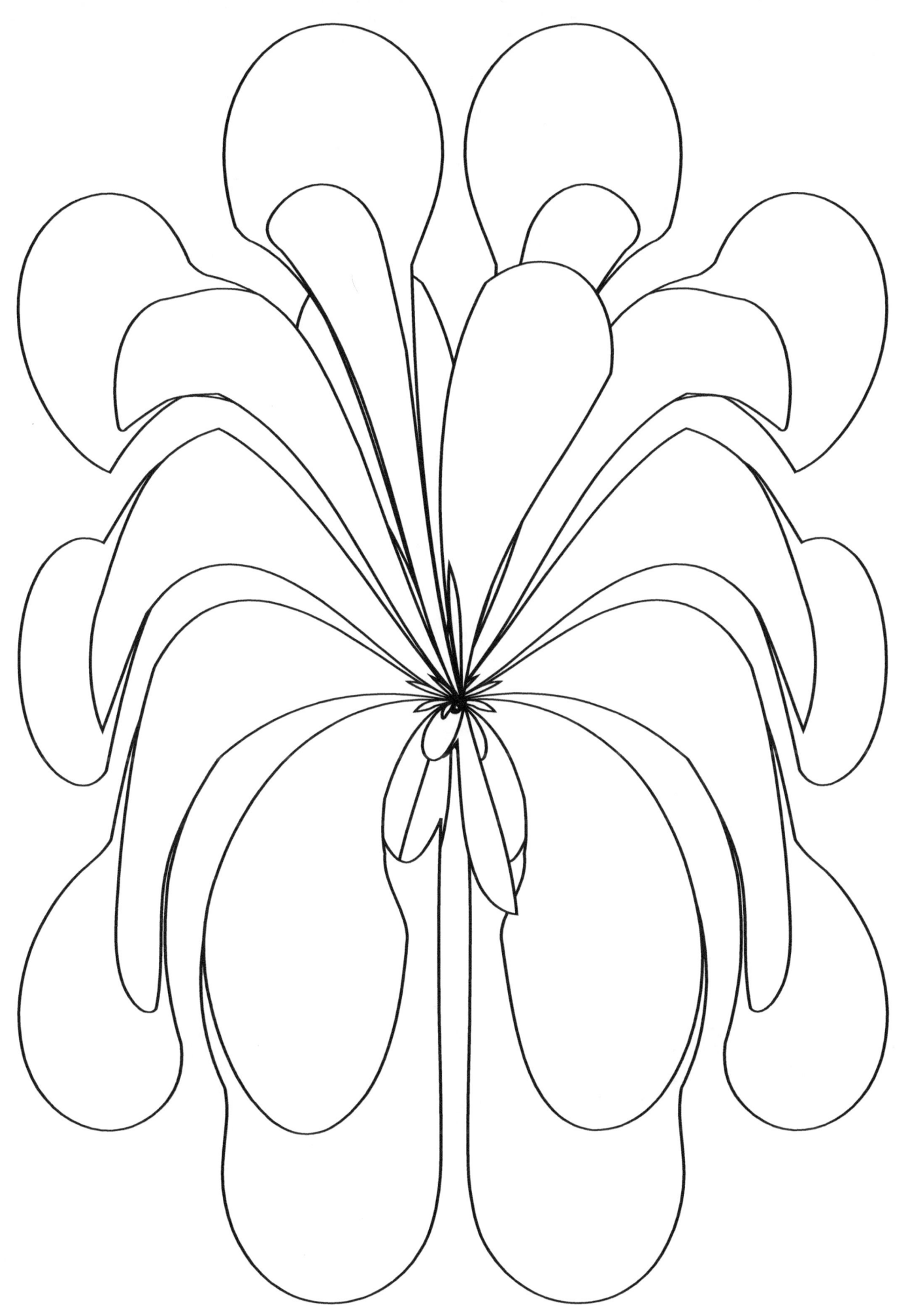

D# 1698

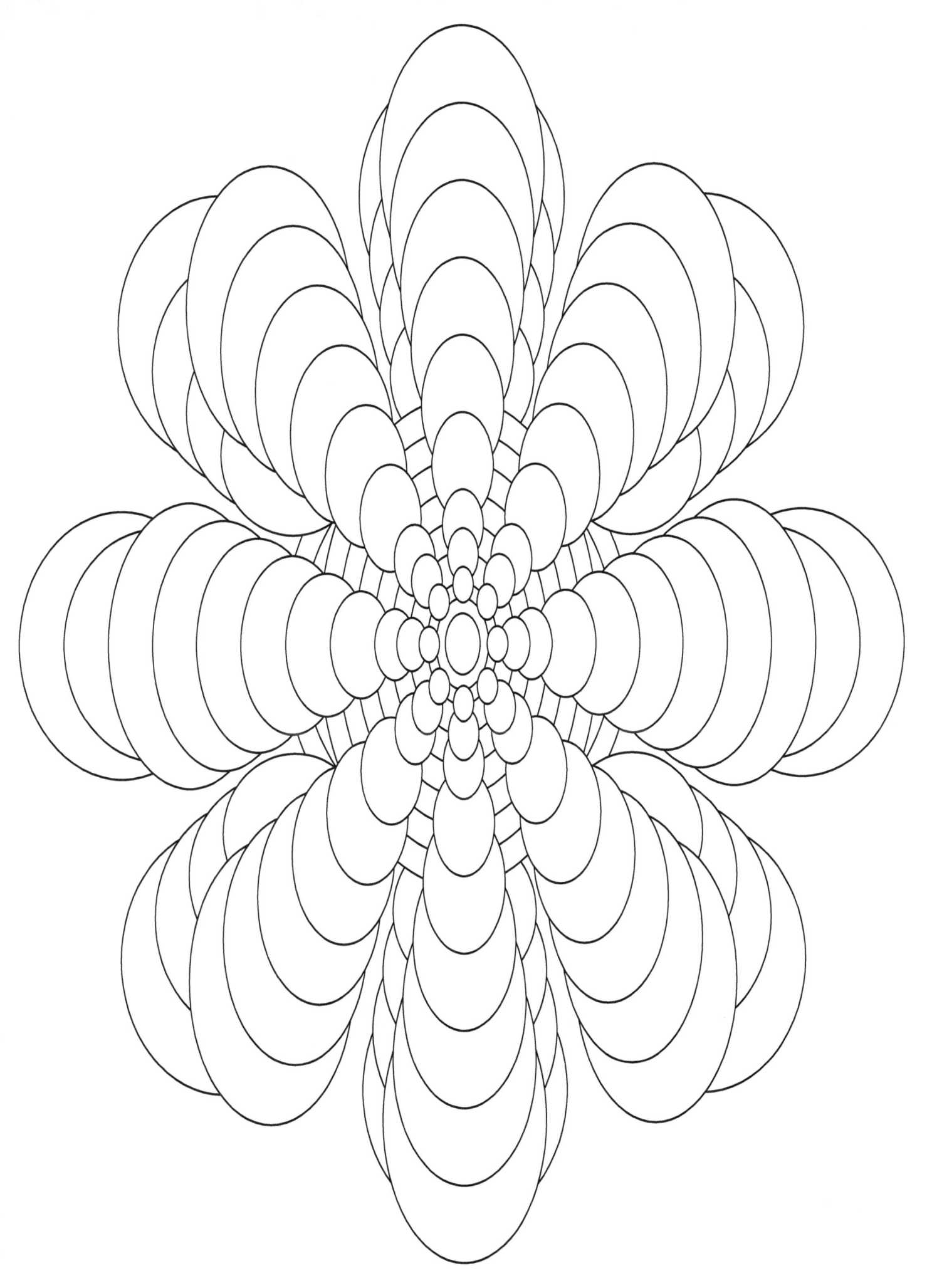

D# 1754

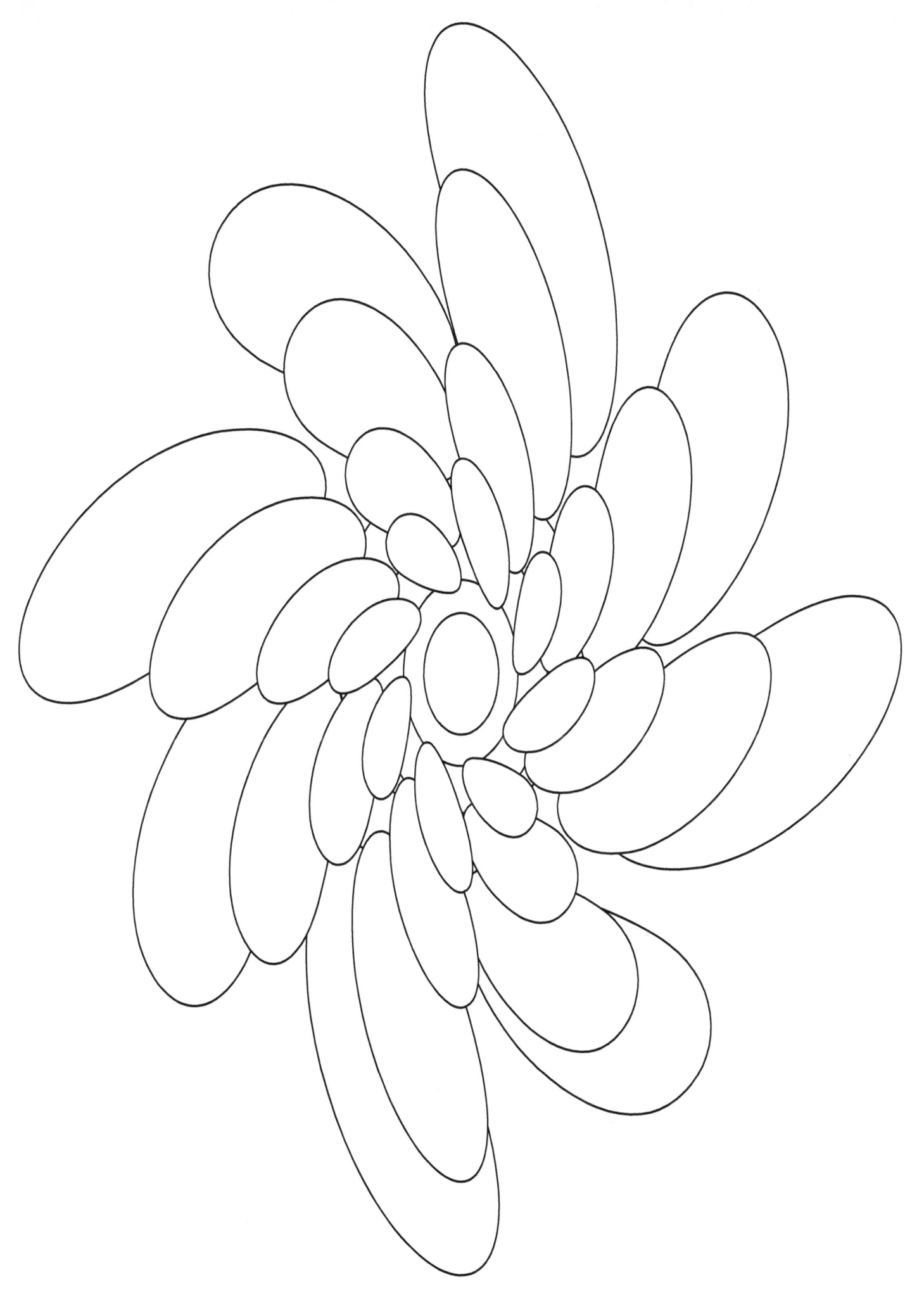

D# 1761

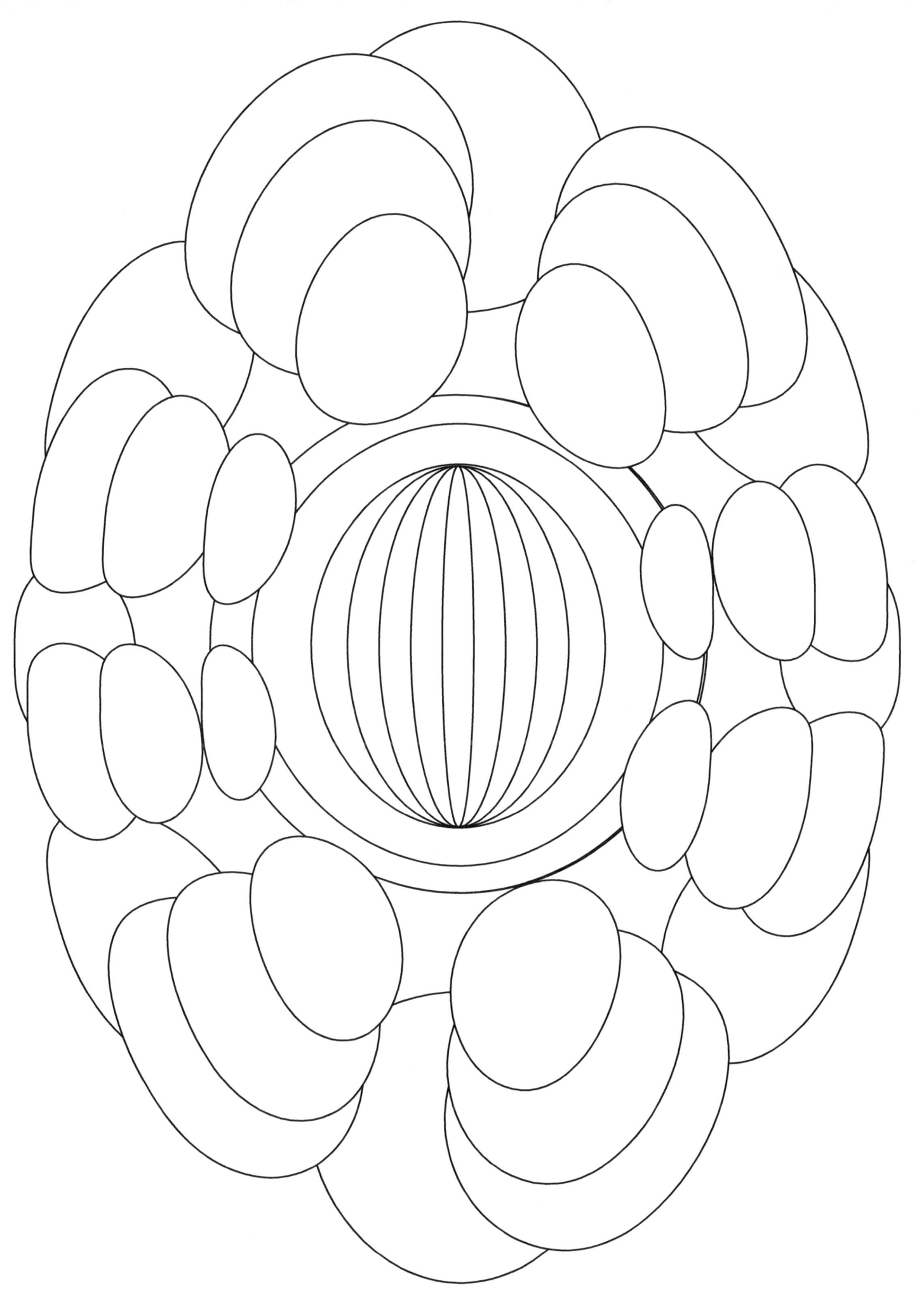

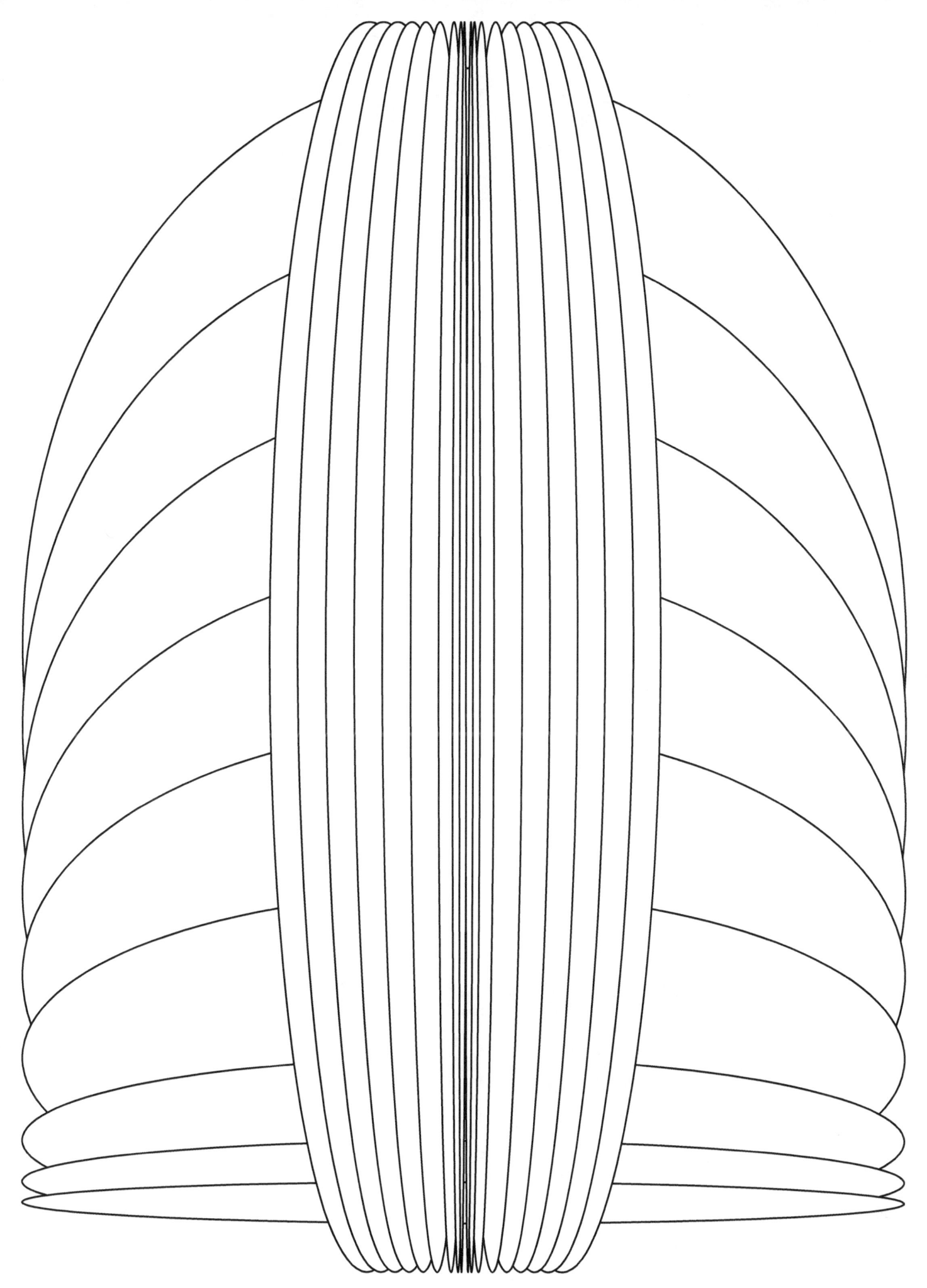

D# 1842

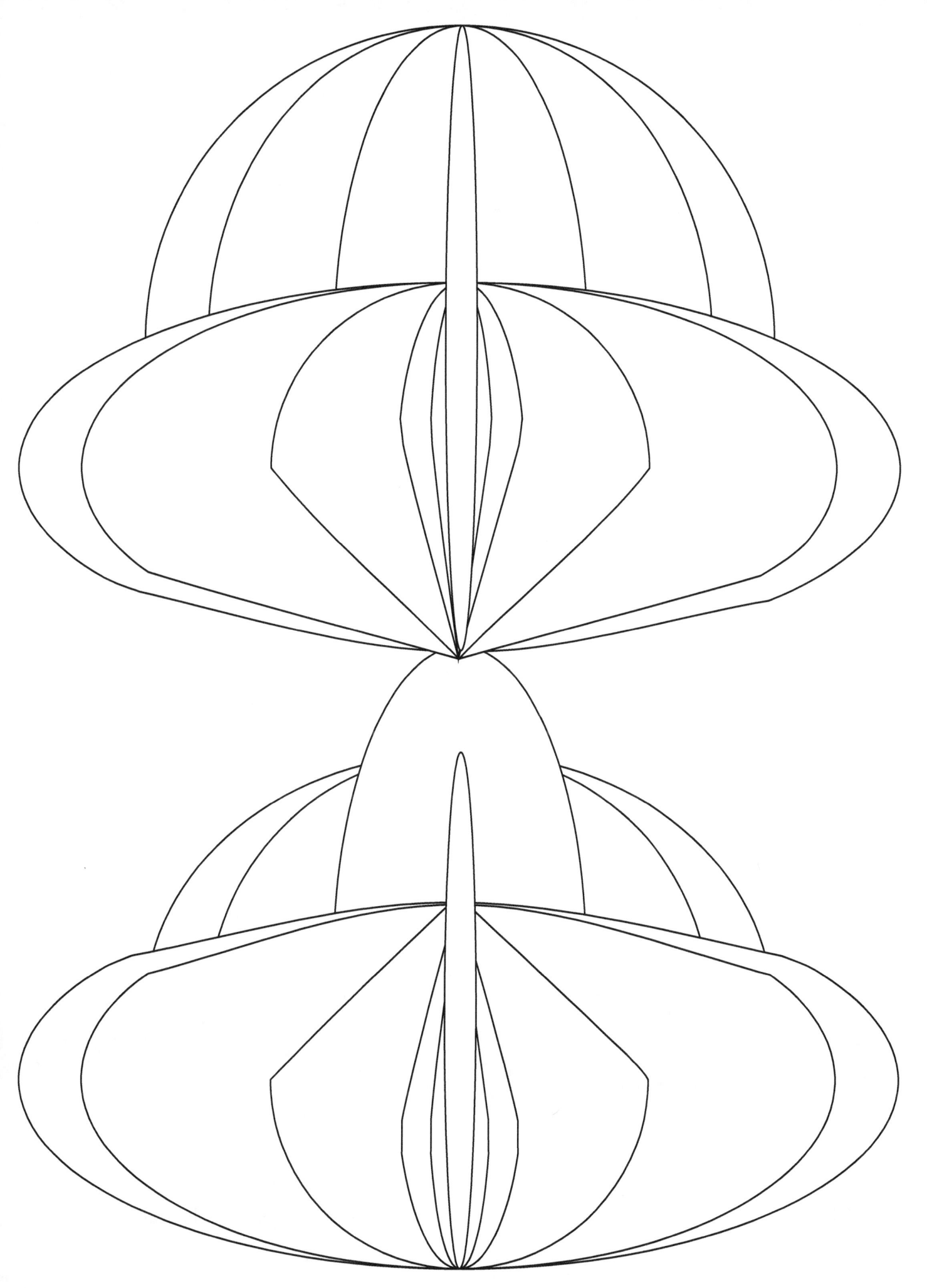

D# 1749

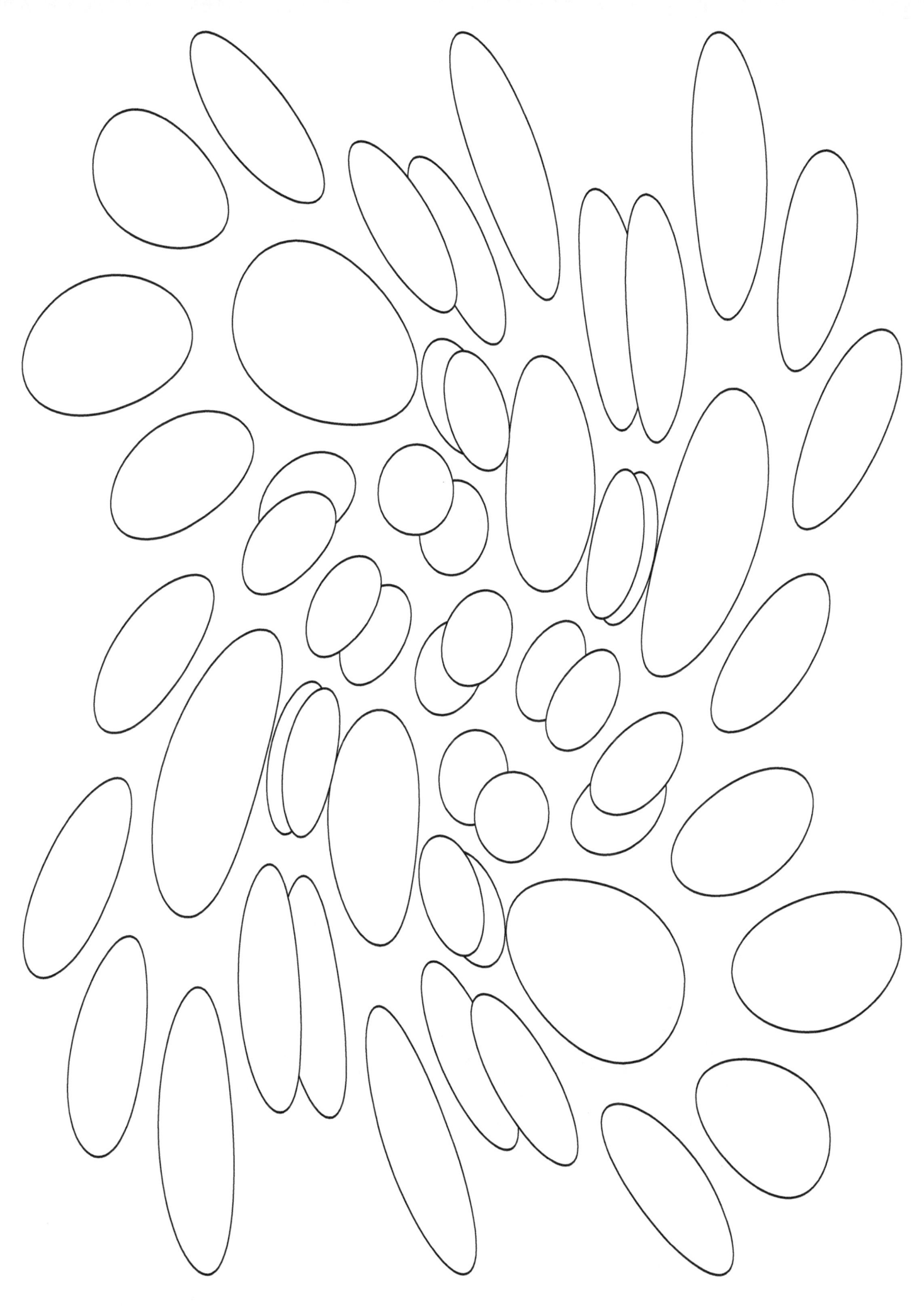

D# 1715

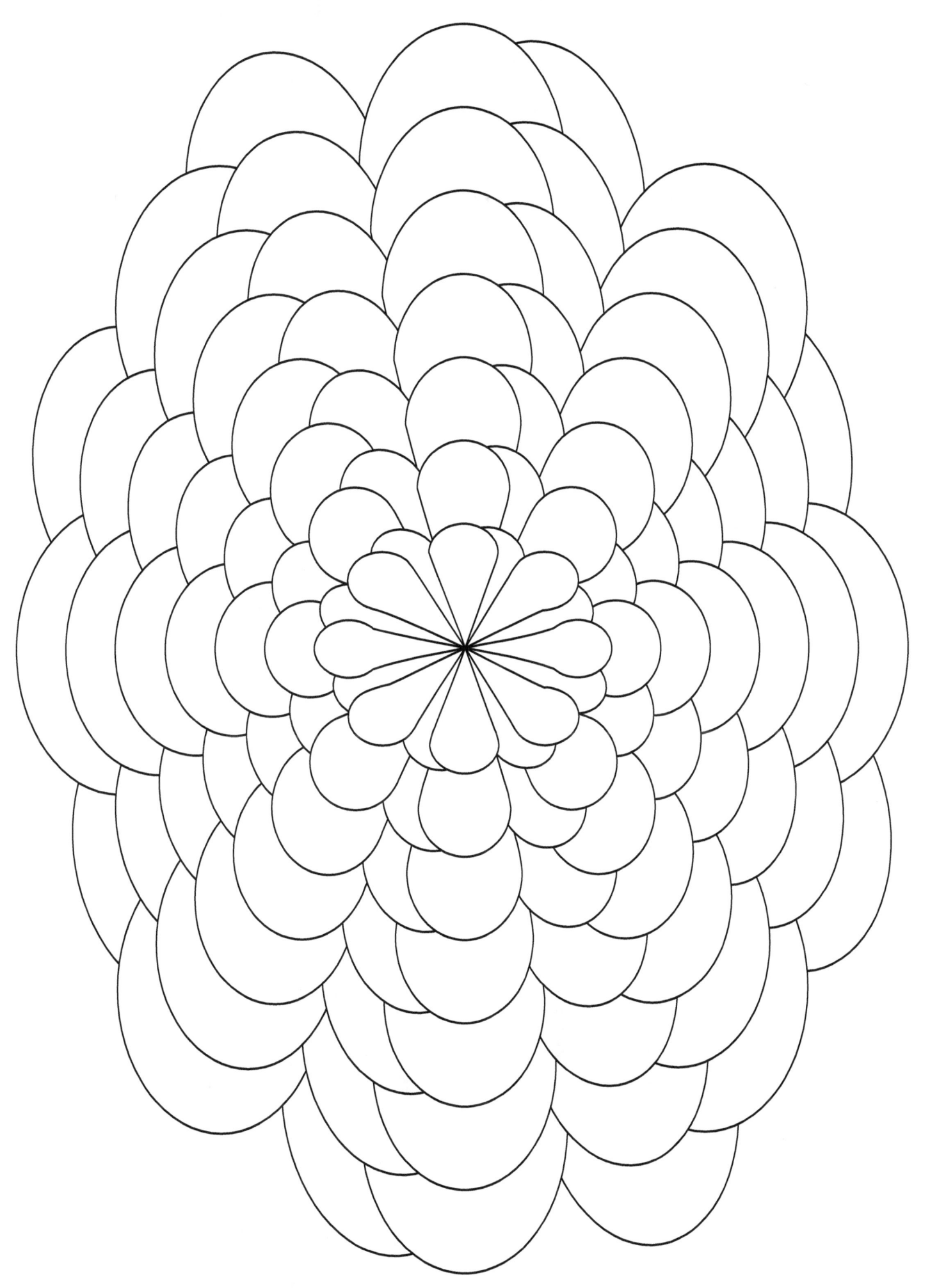

D# 1835

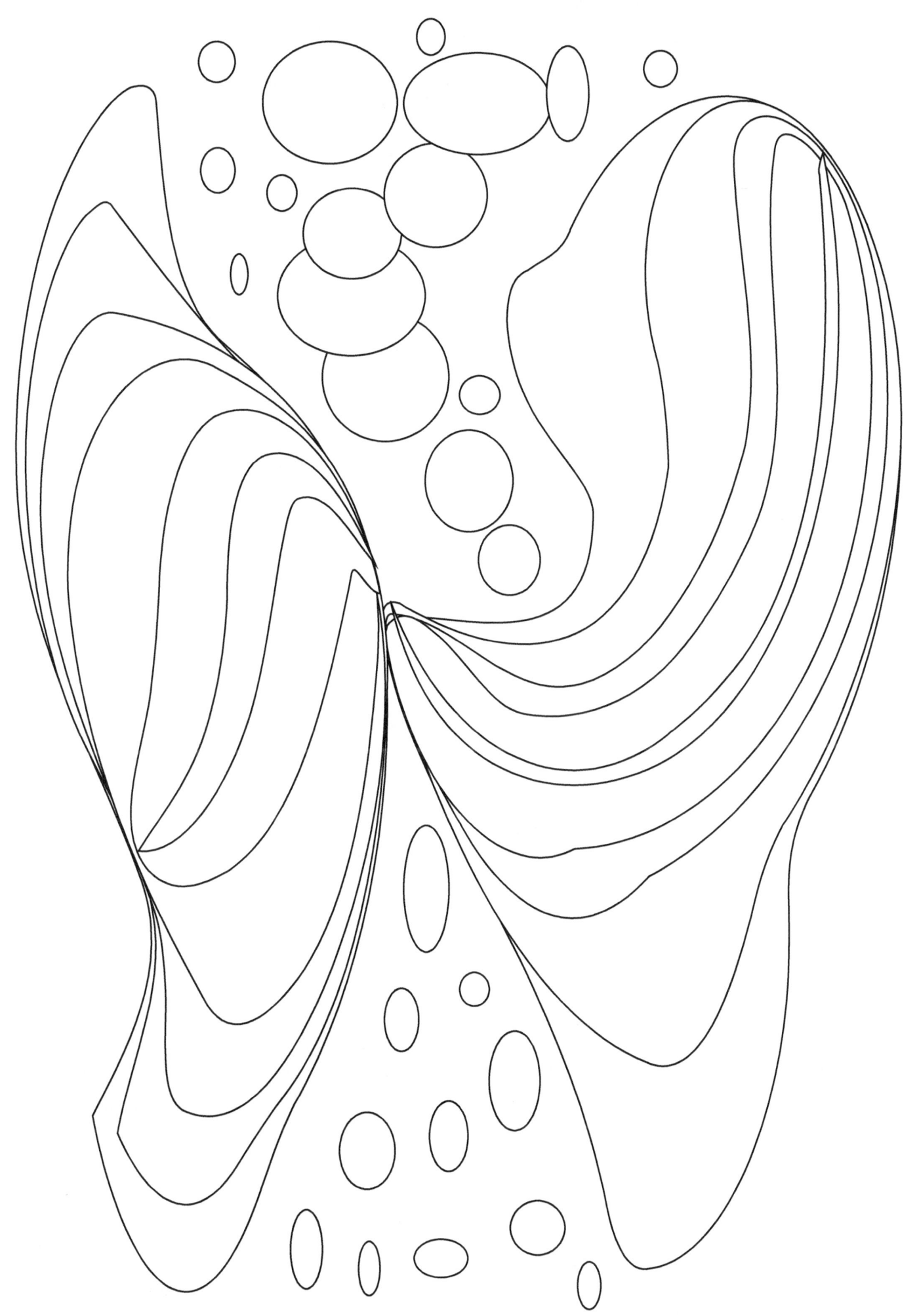

D# 1712

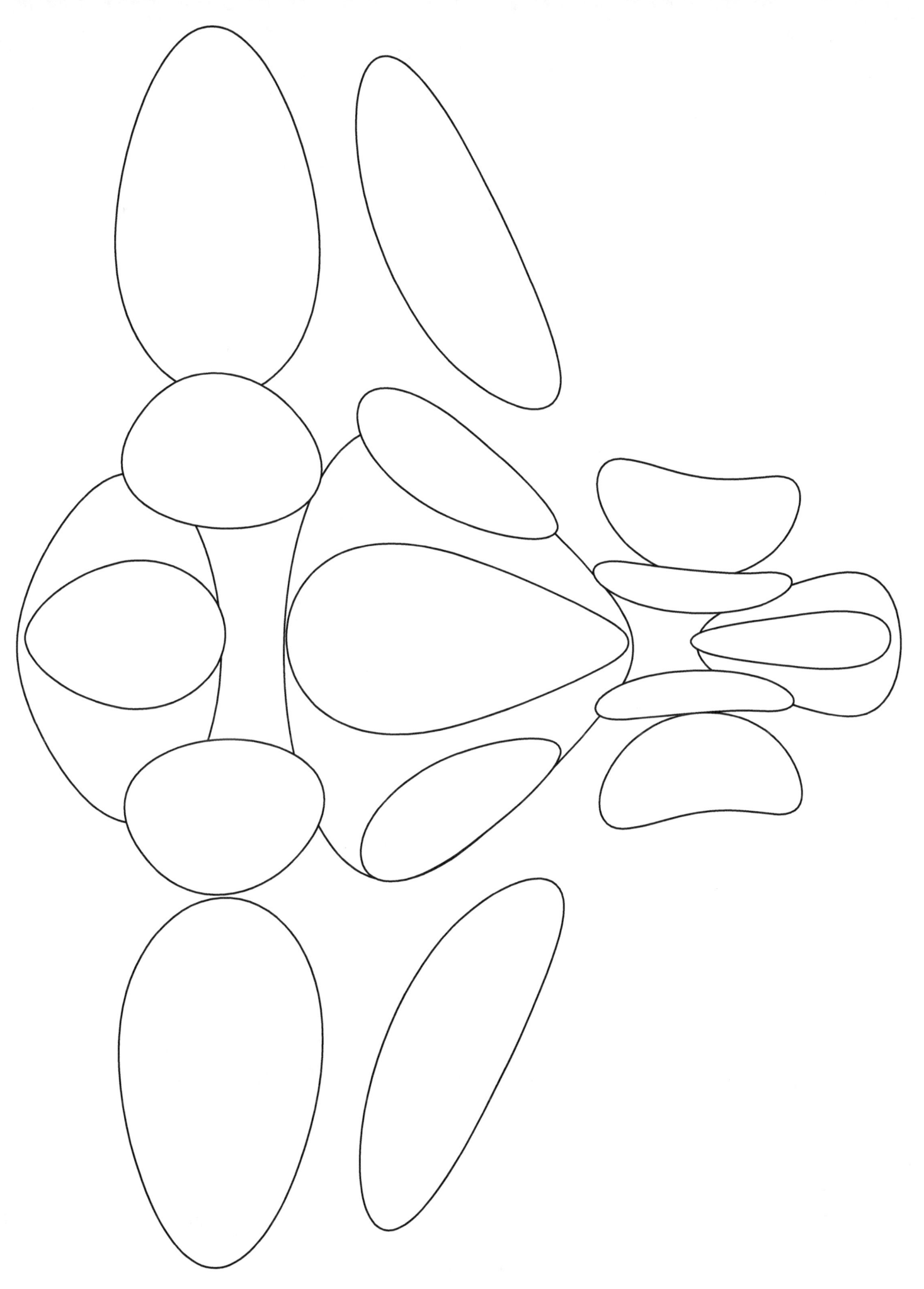

D# 1841

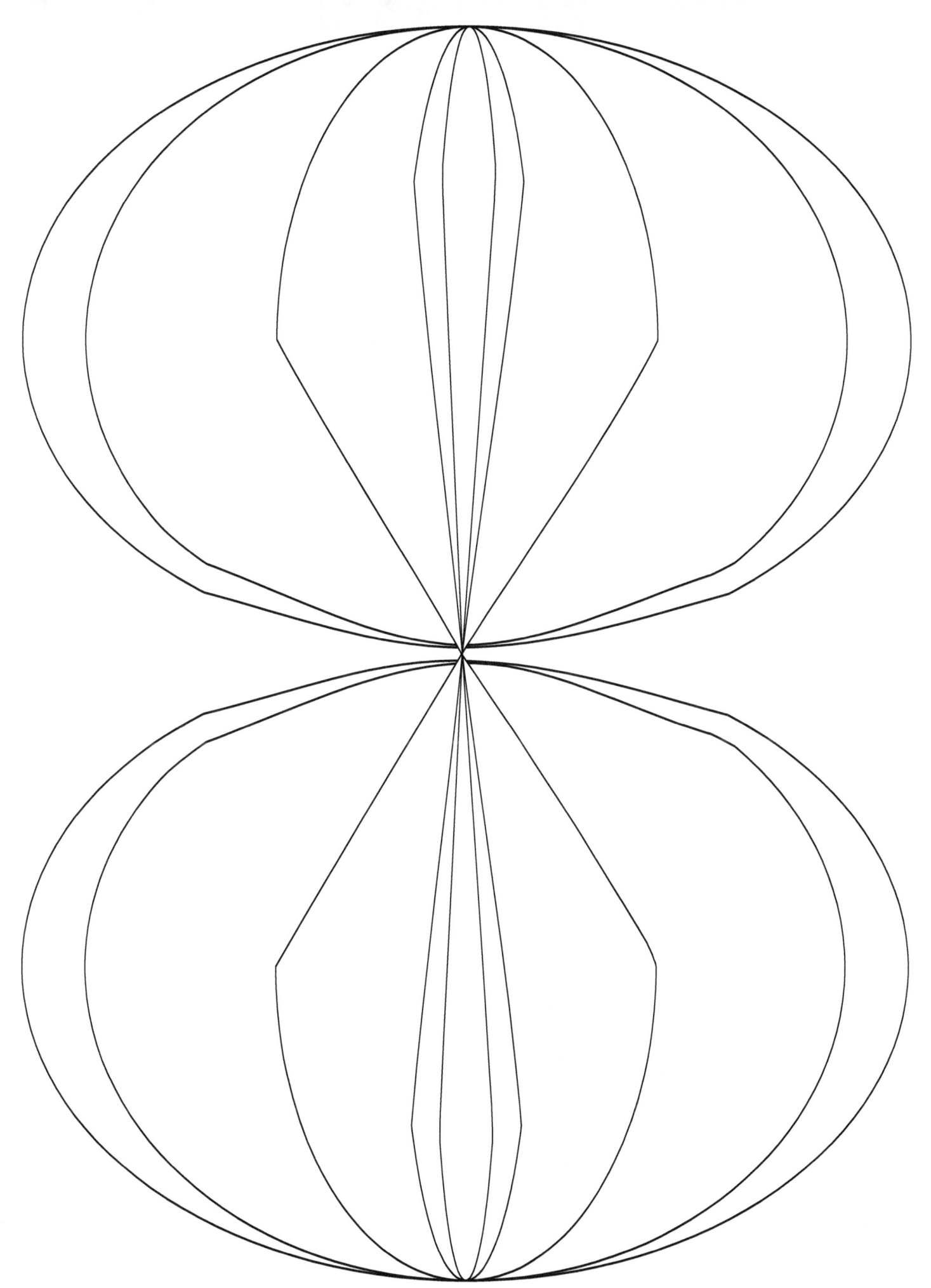

D# 1729

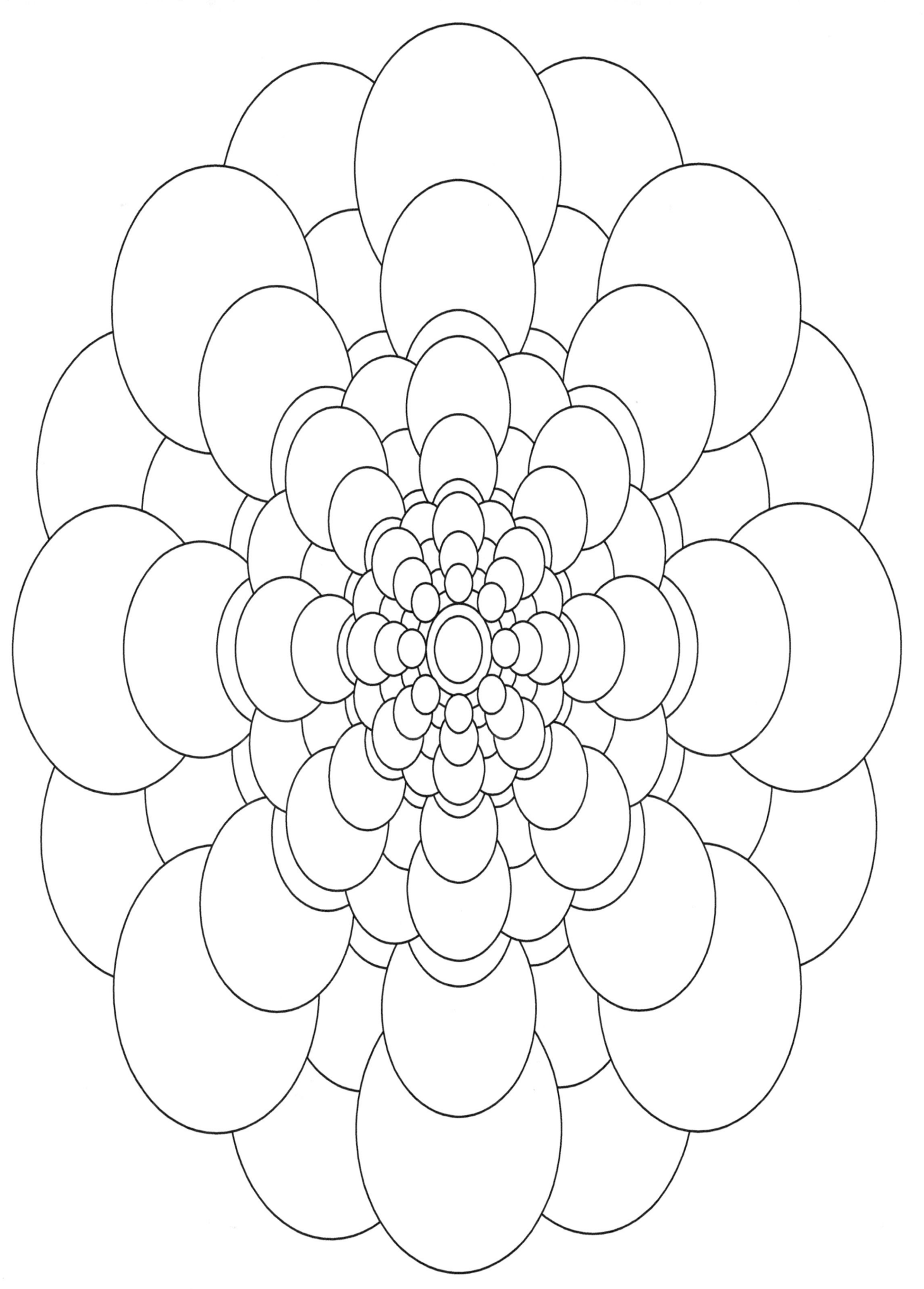

D# 1728

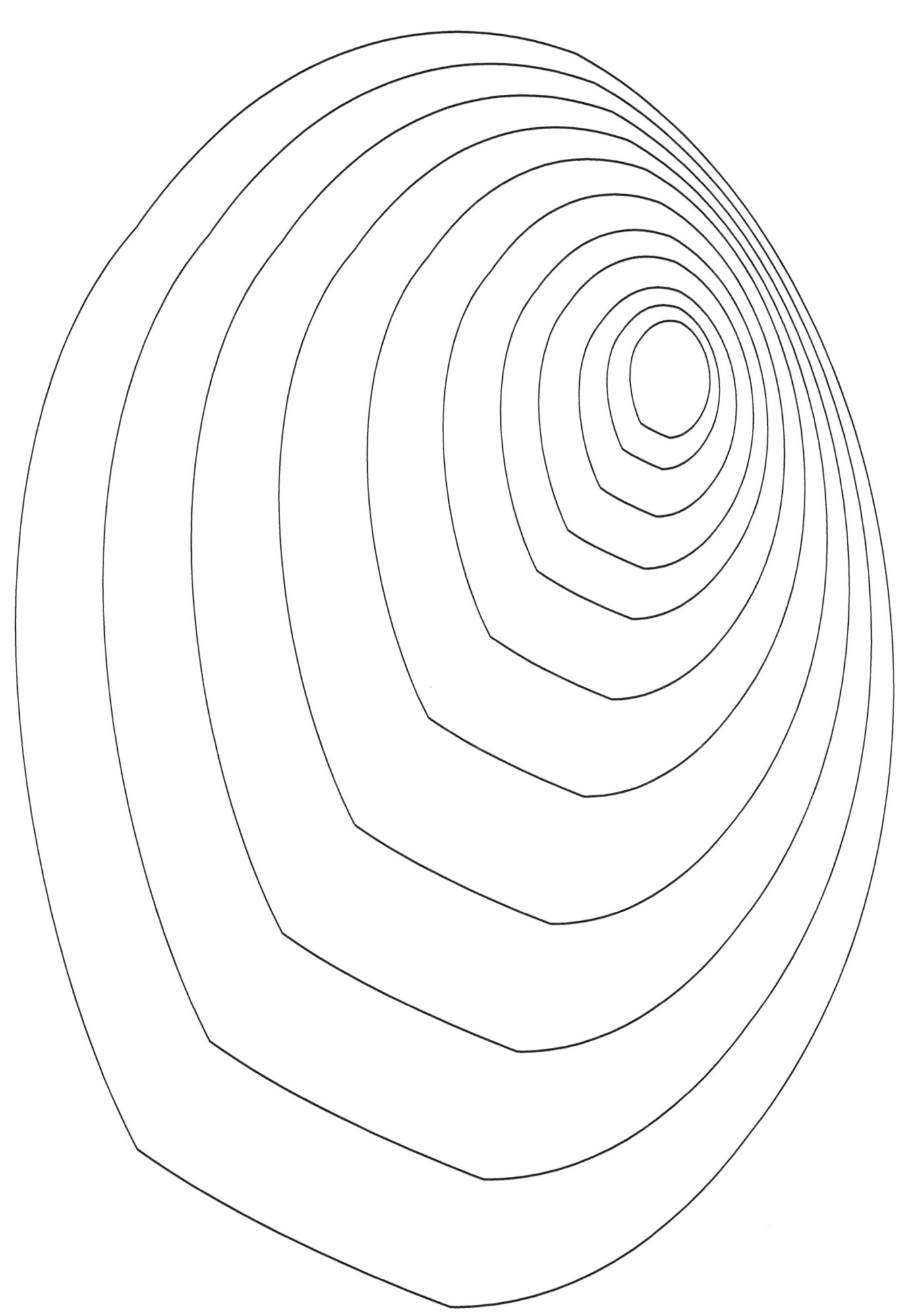

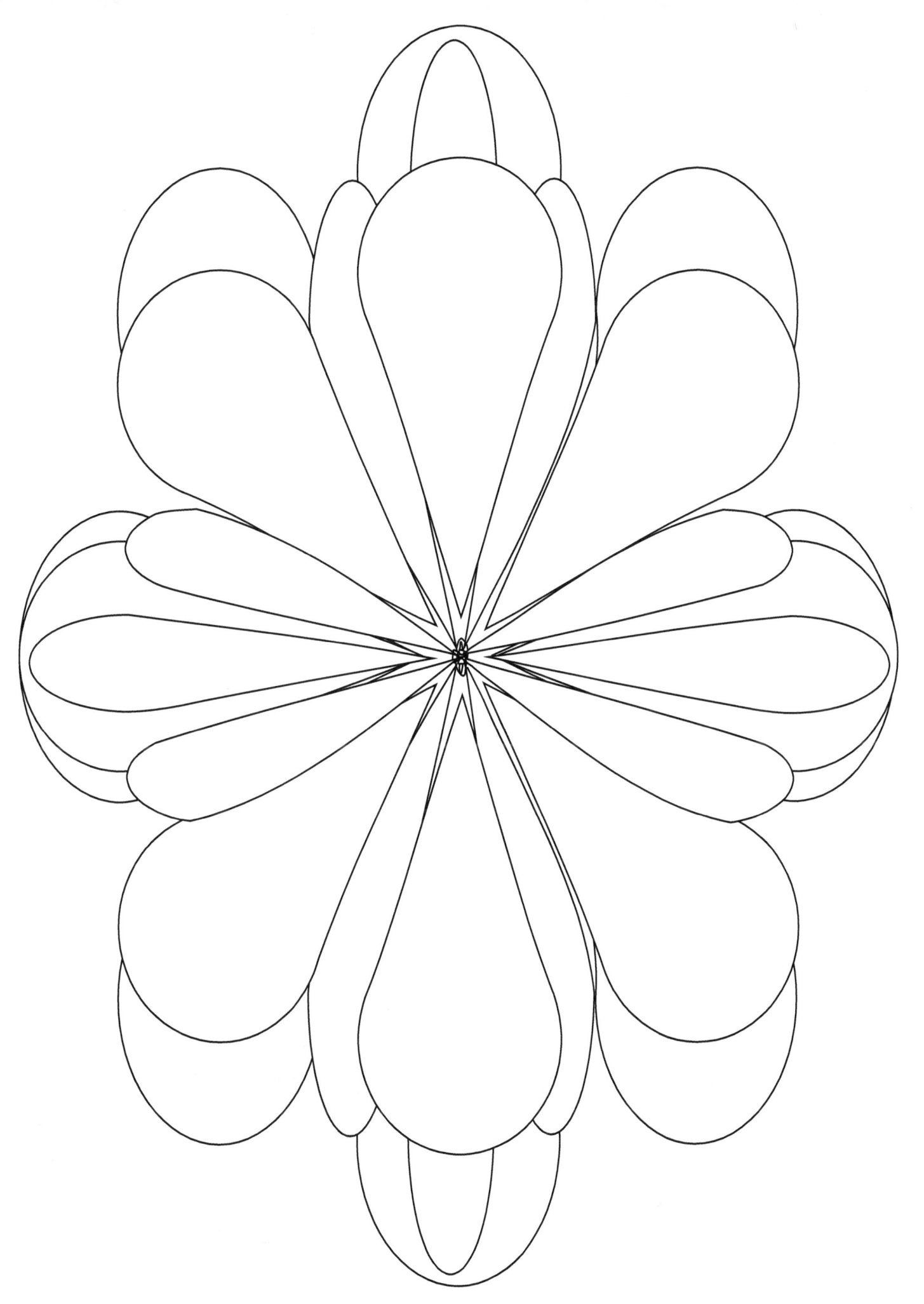

D# 1705

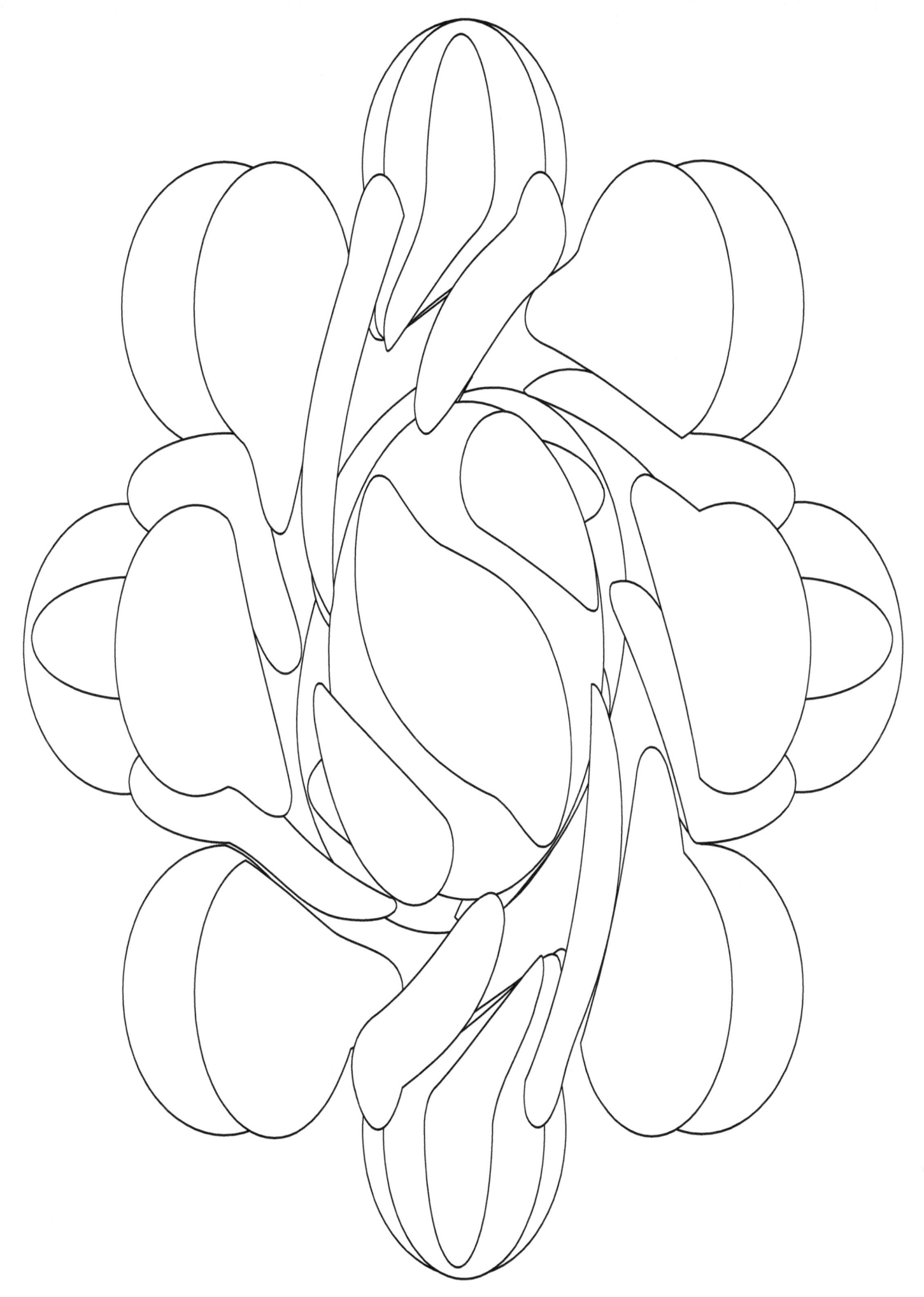

D# 1731

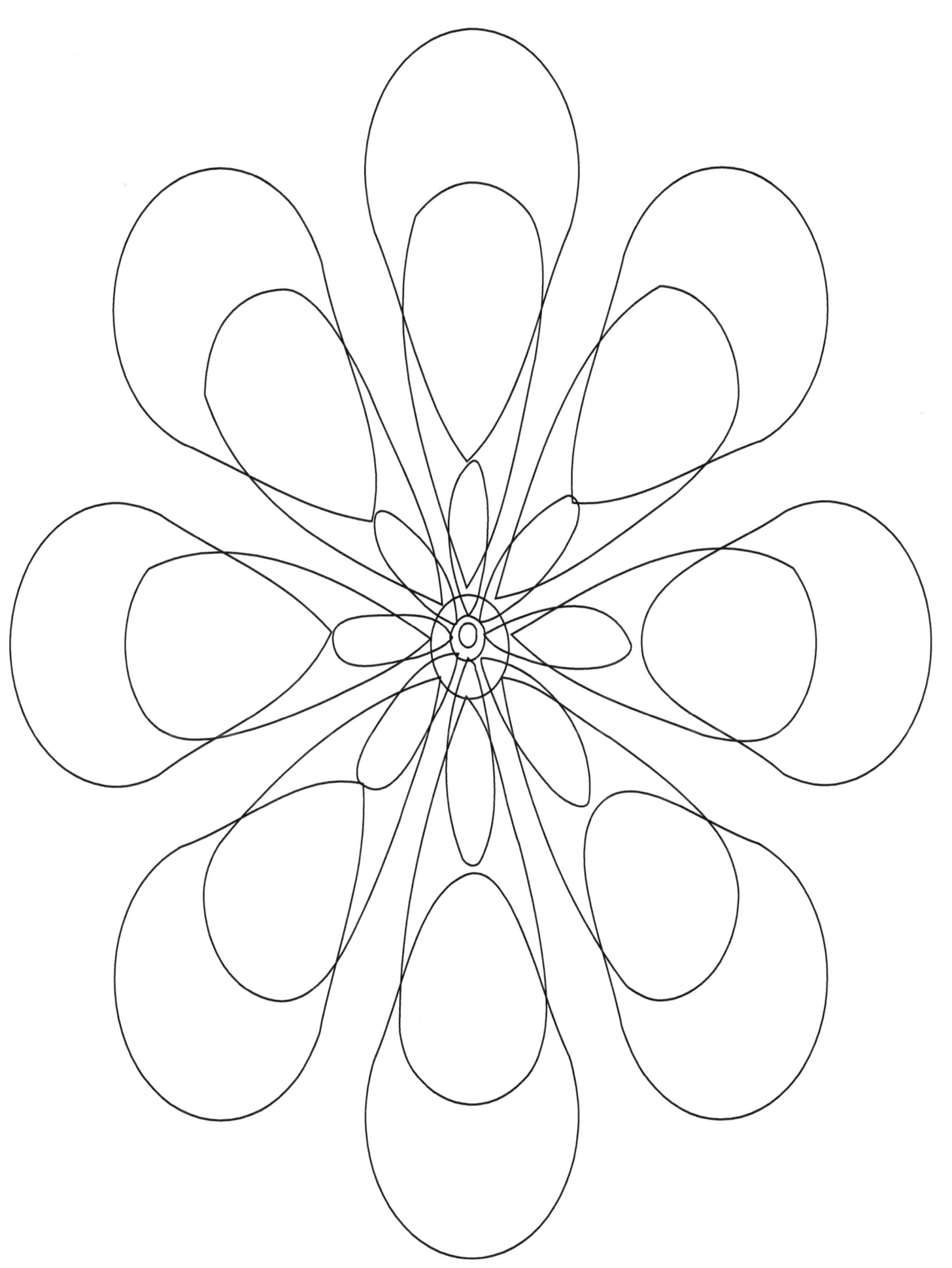

D# 1702

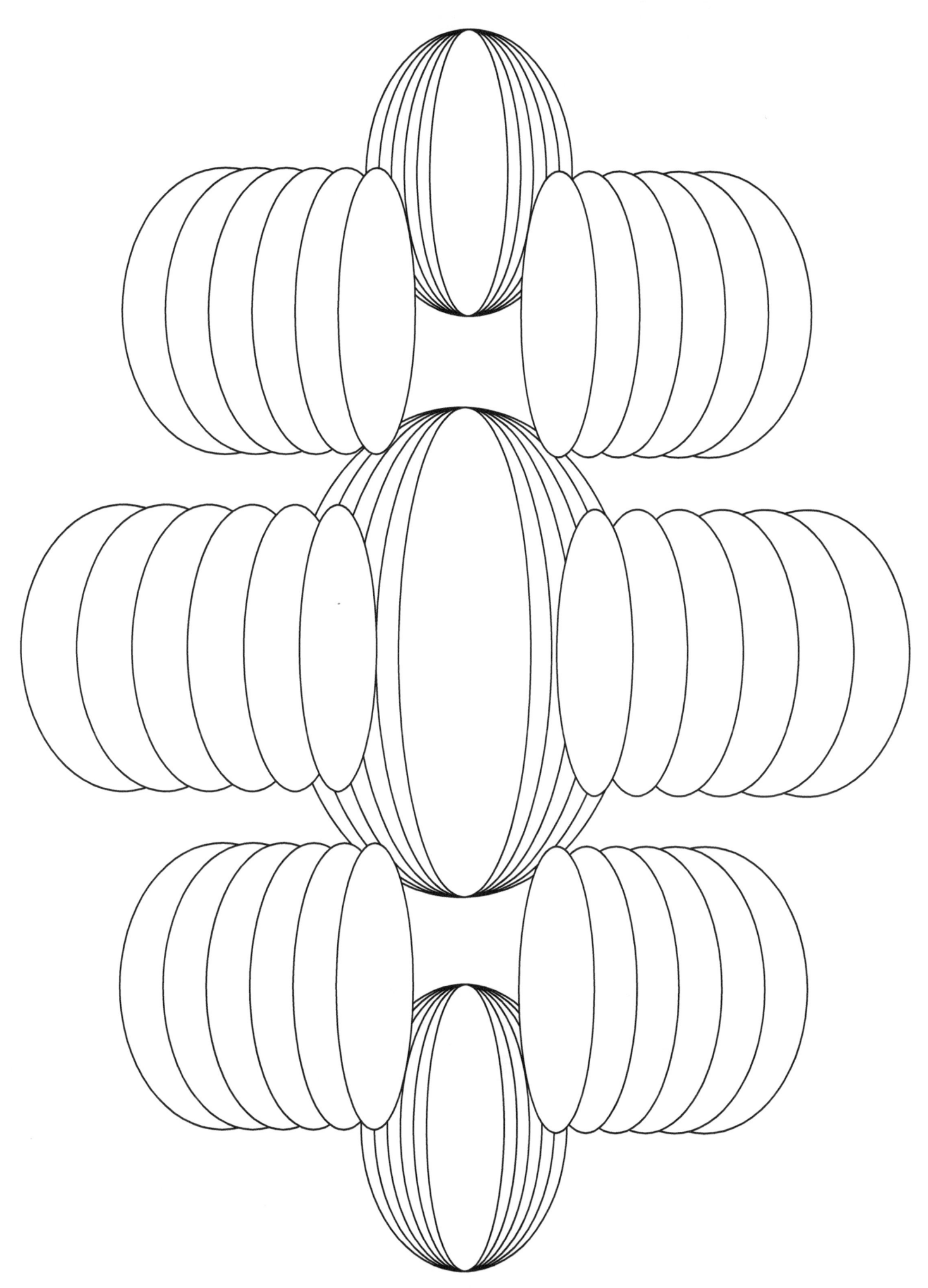

D# 1807

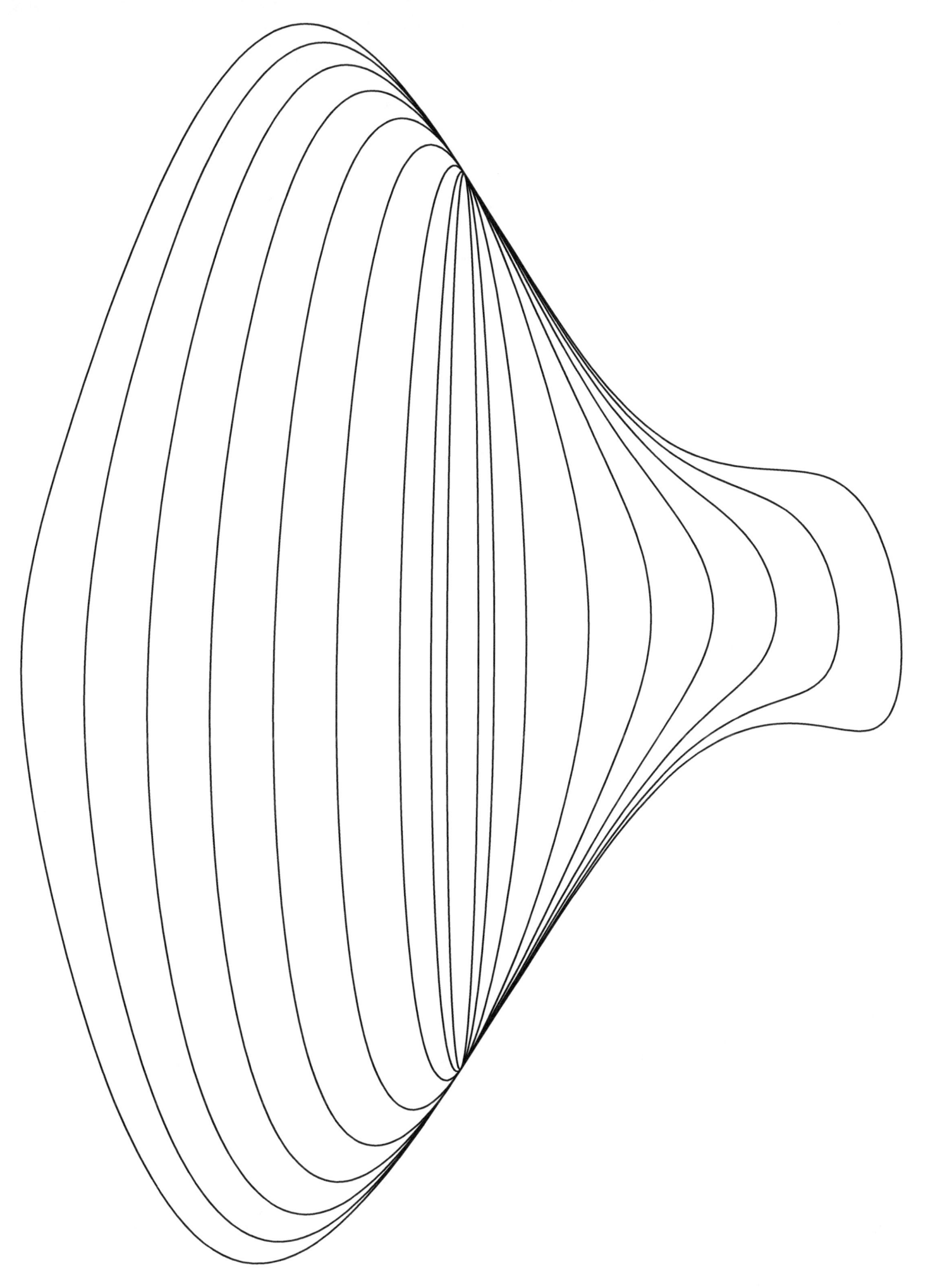

D# 1704

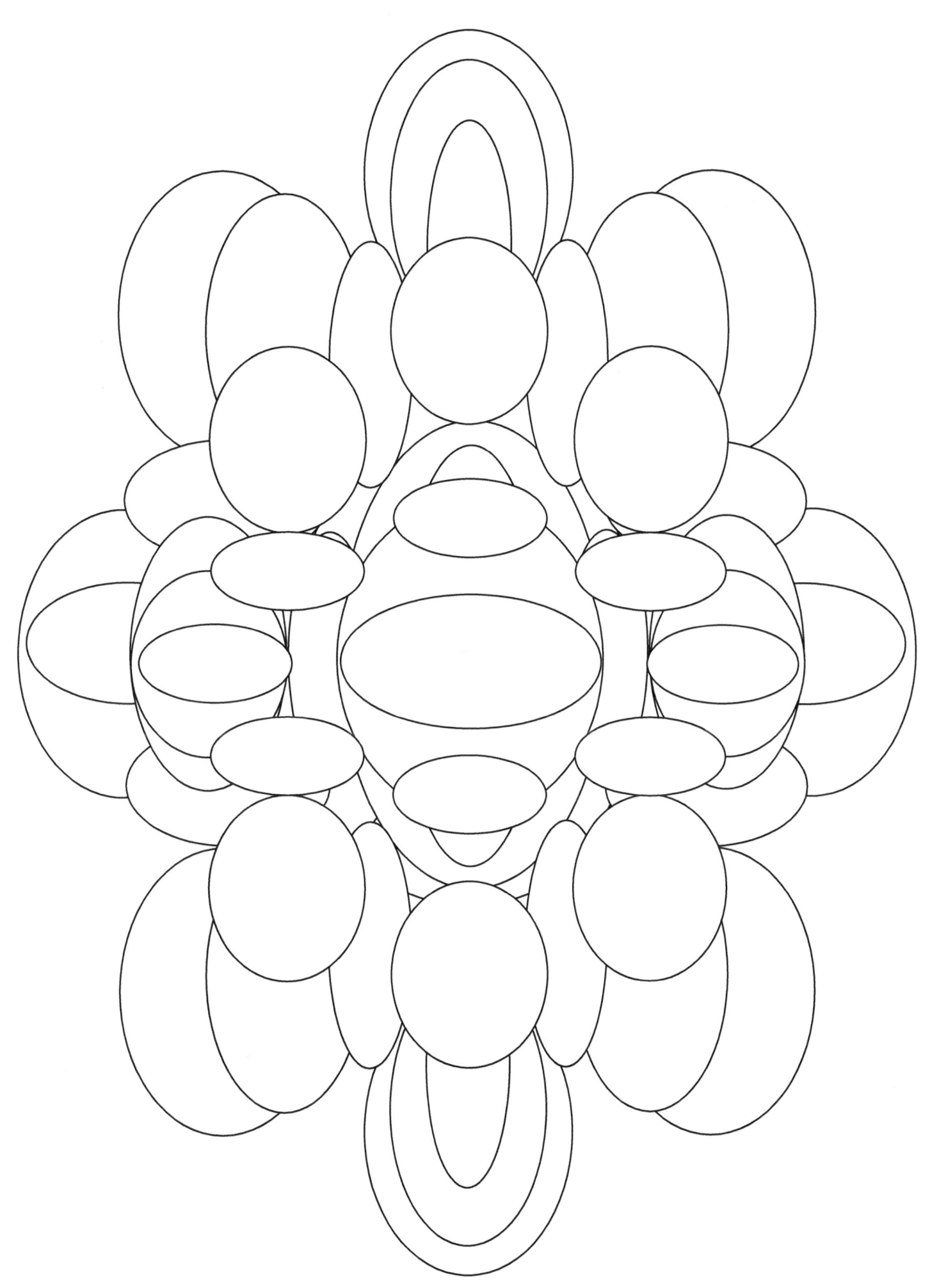

D# 1686

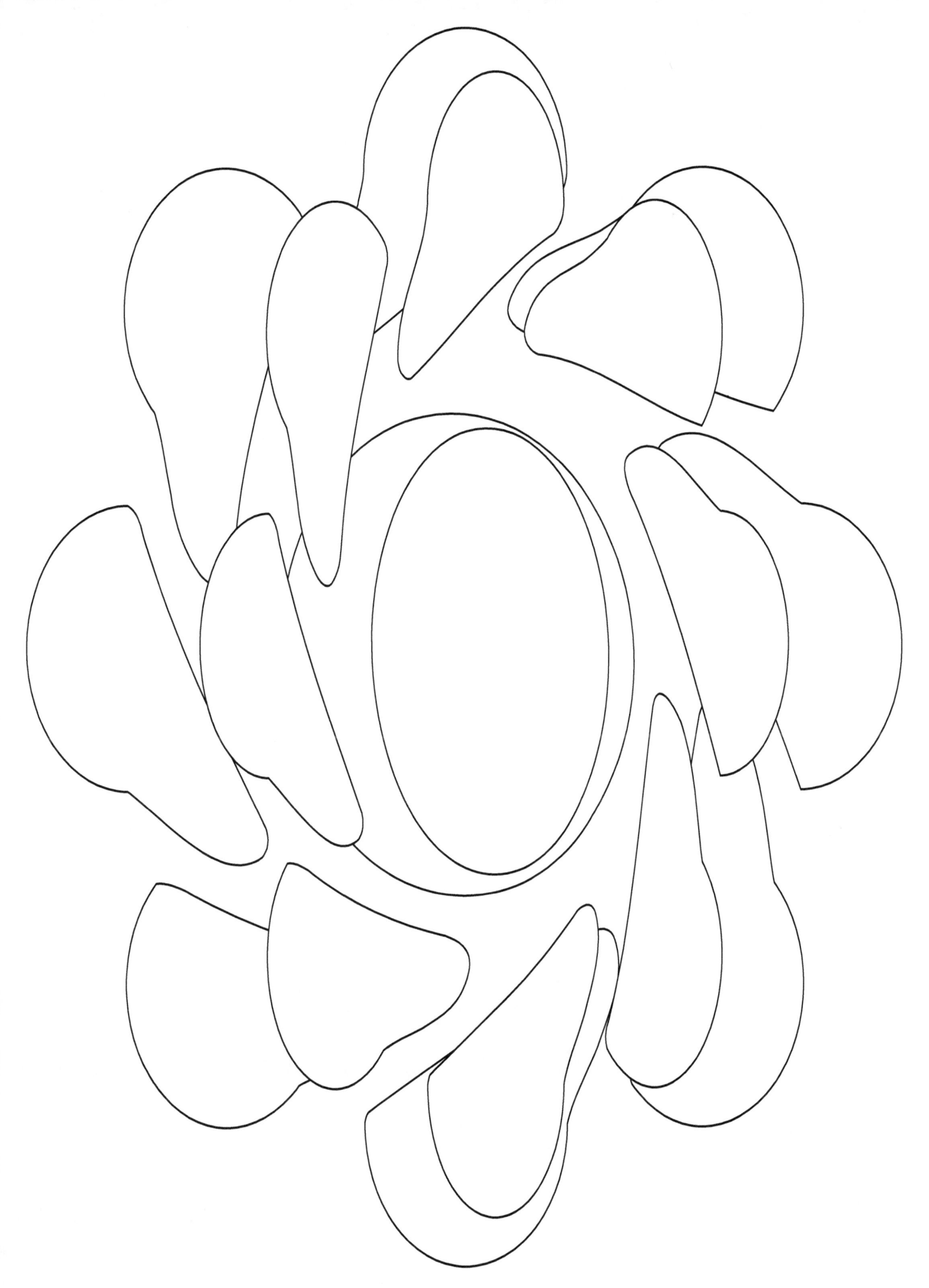

D# 1691

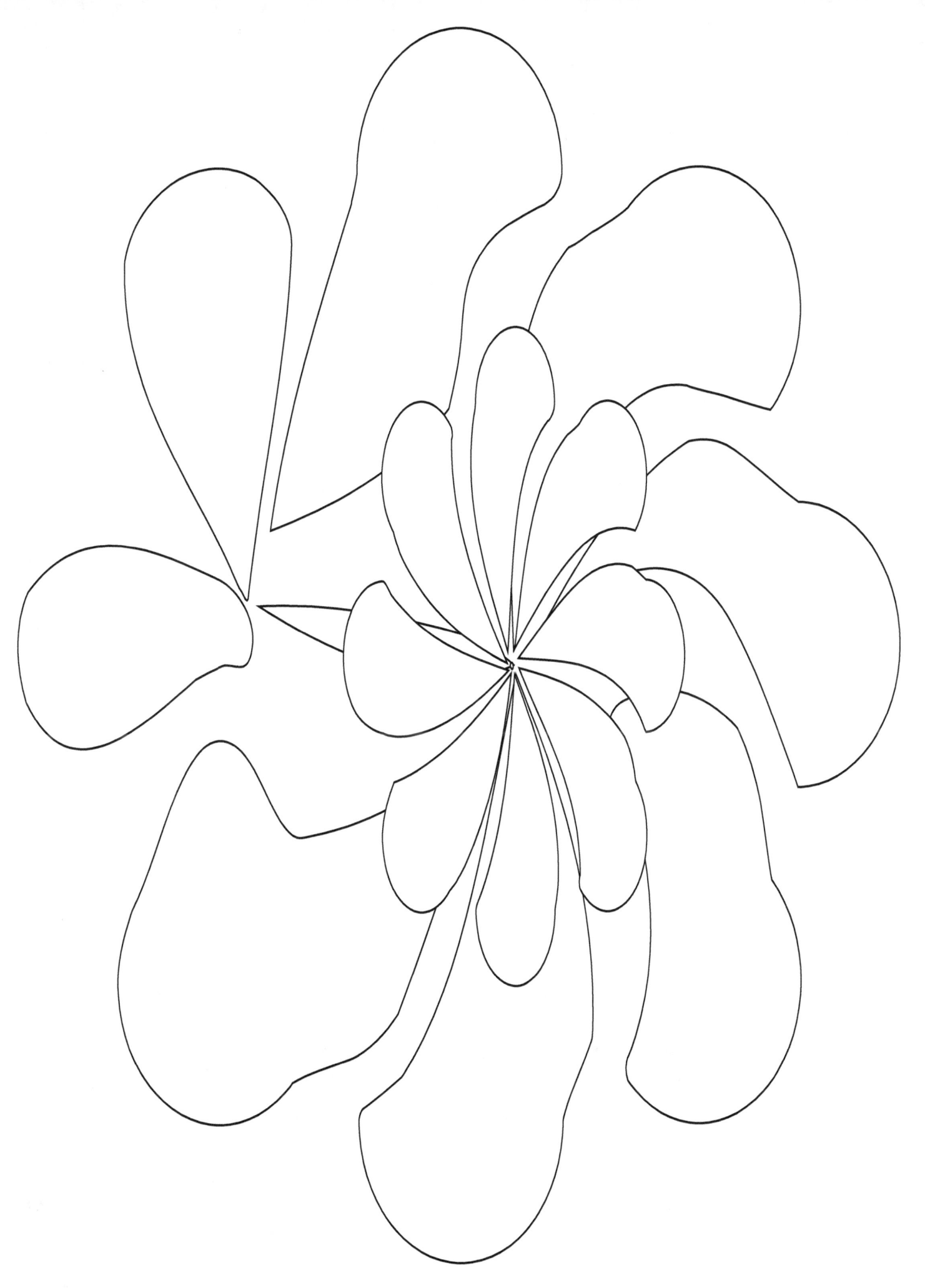

D# 1766

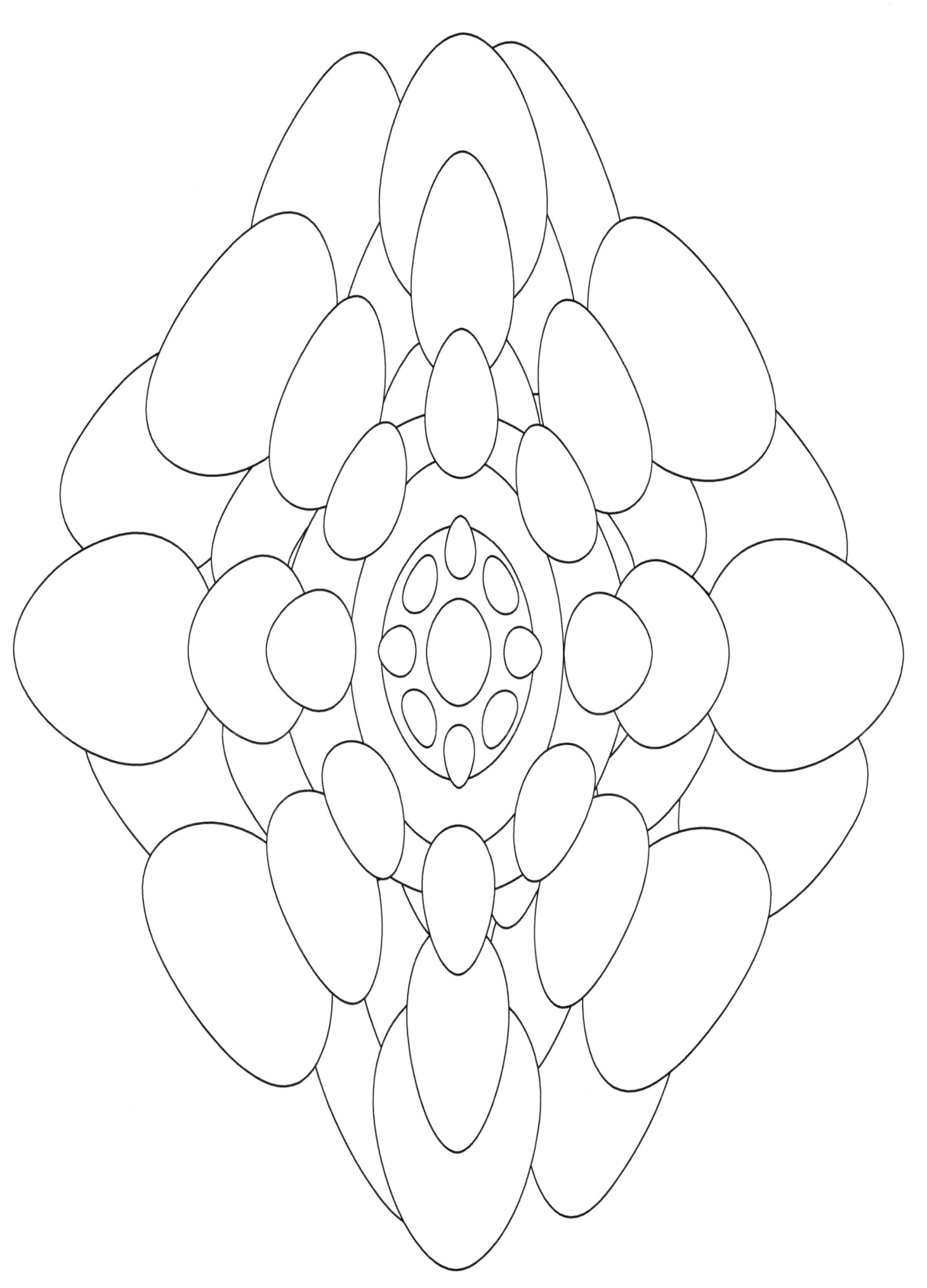

D# 1707

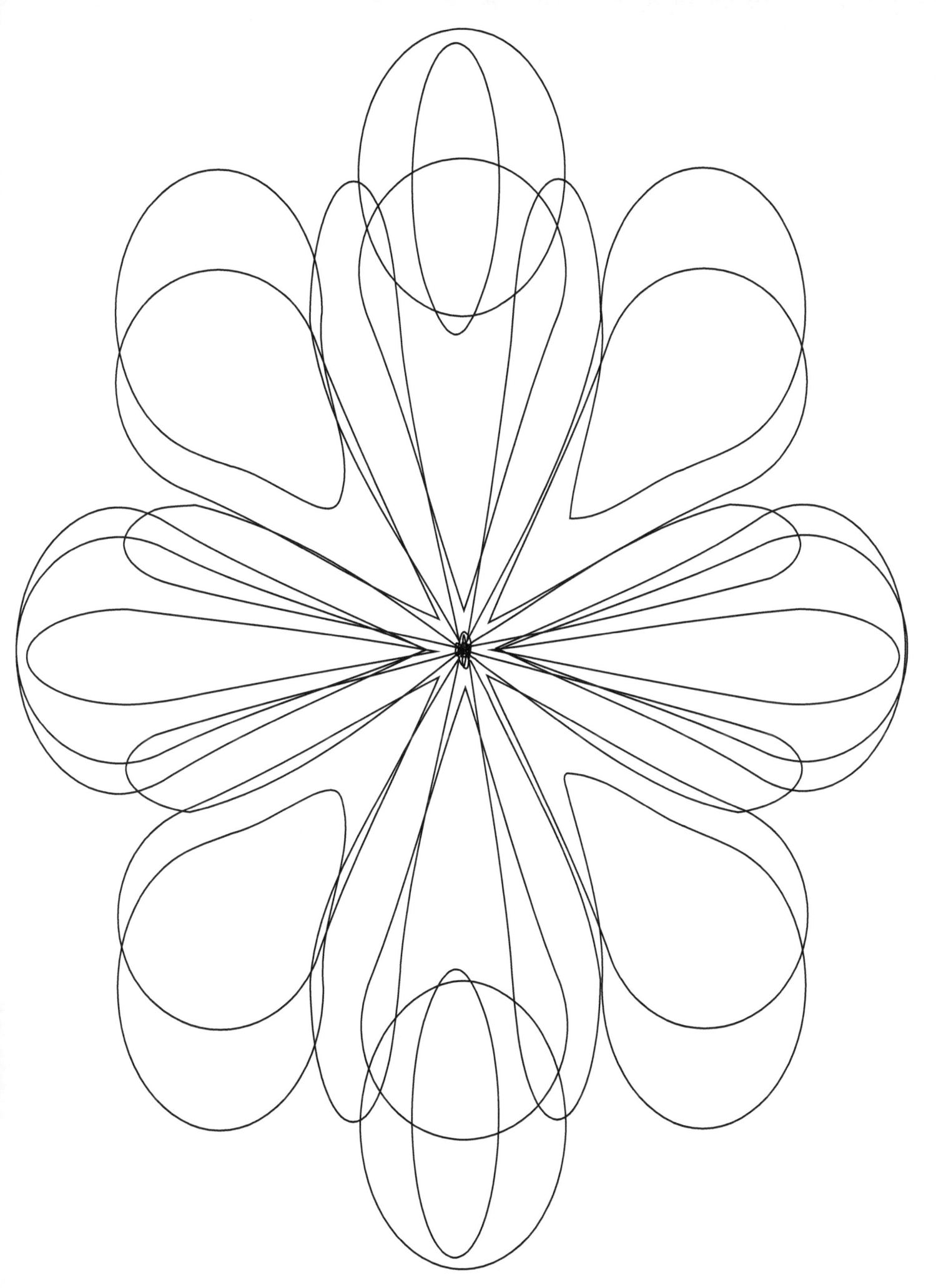

D# 1752

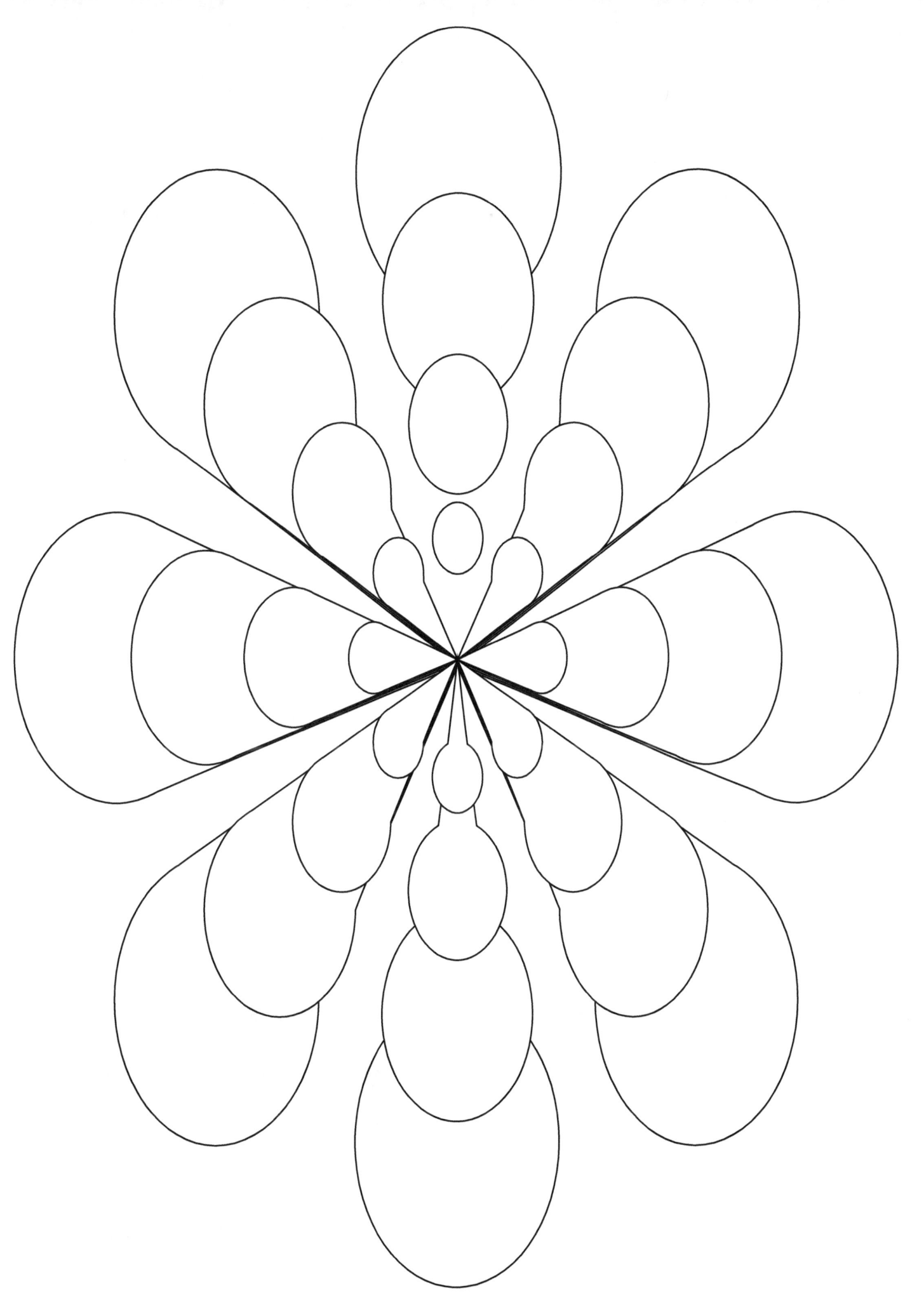

D# 1741

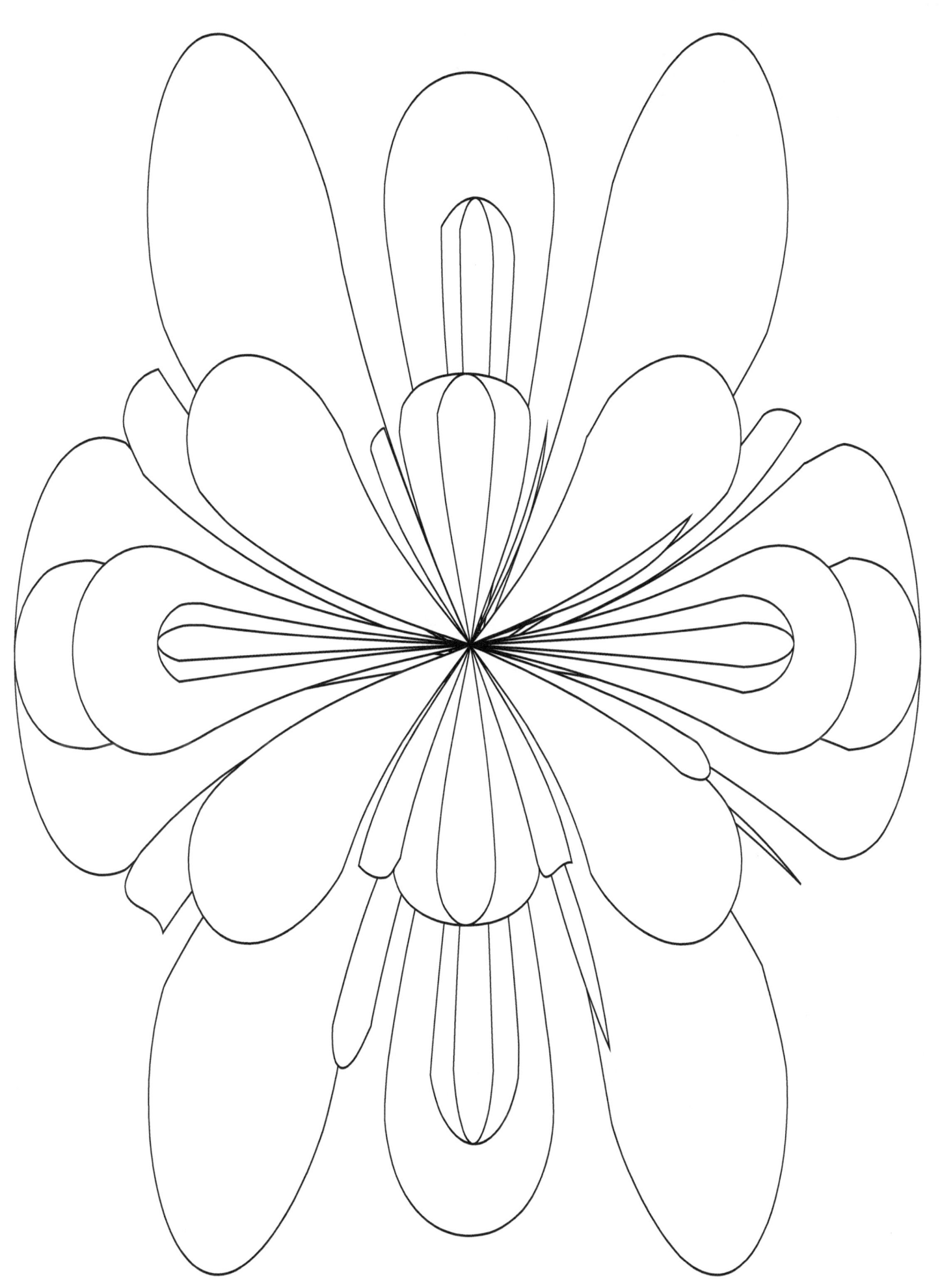

D# 1840

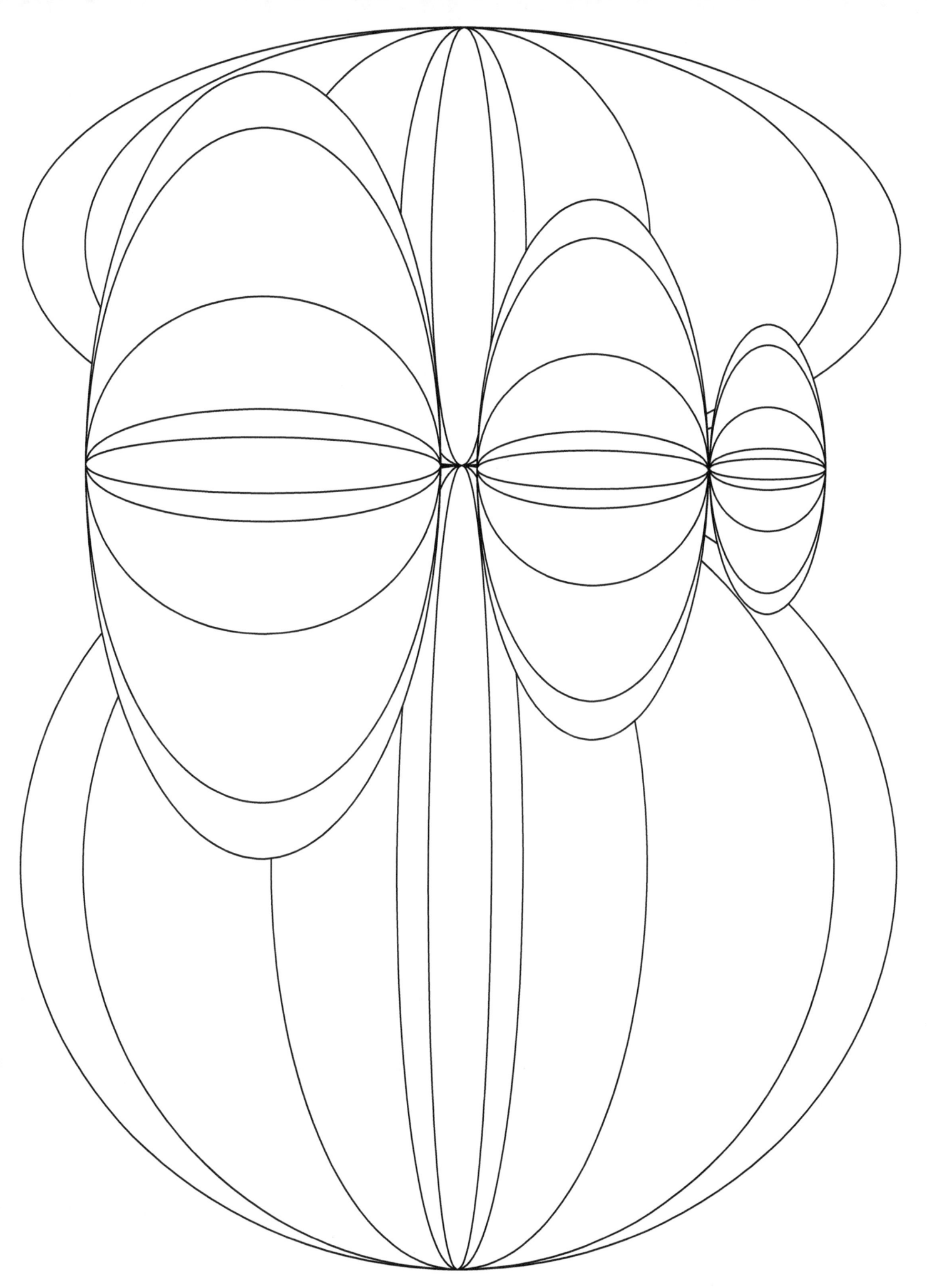

D# 1748

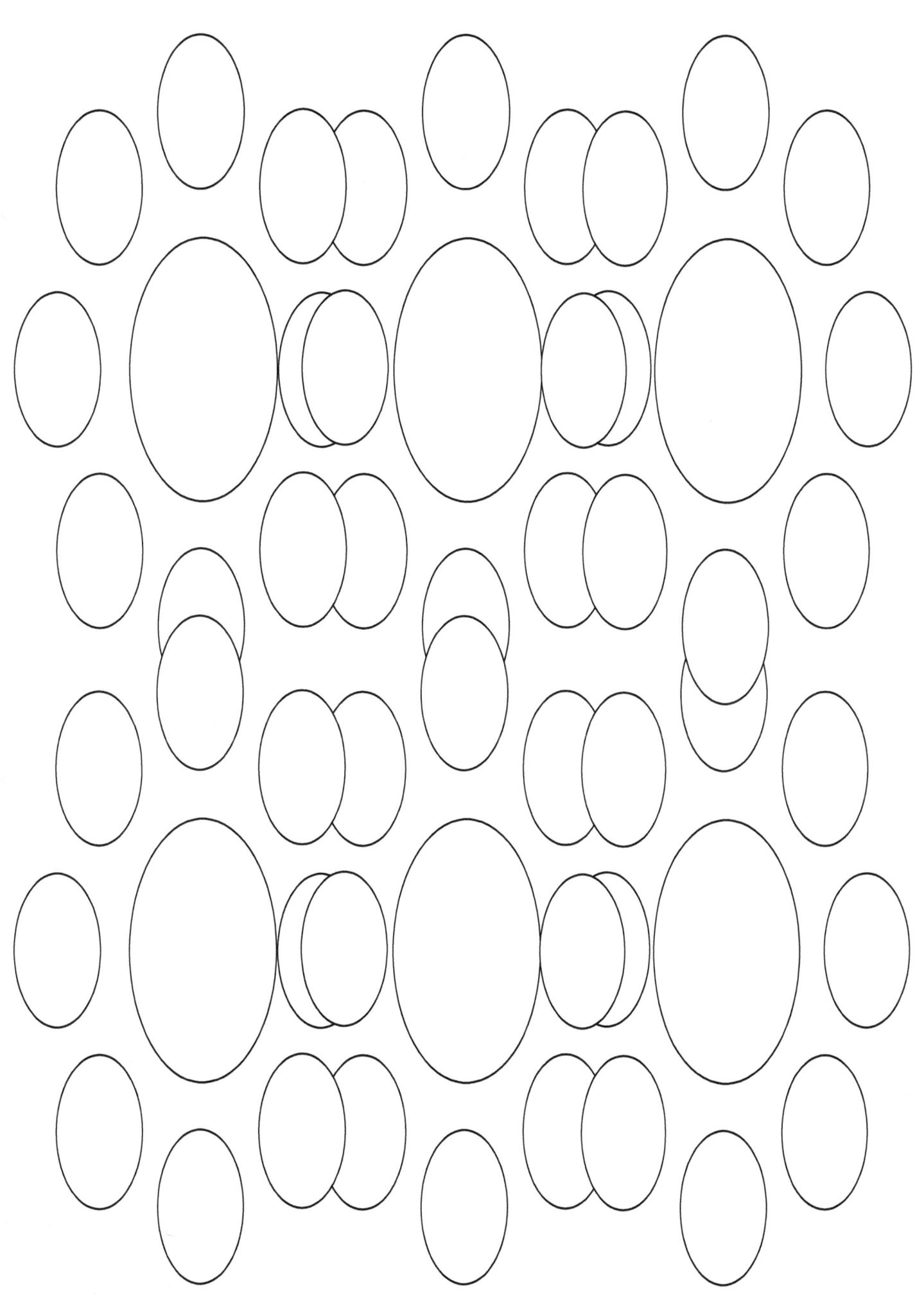

D# 1708

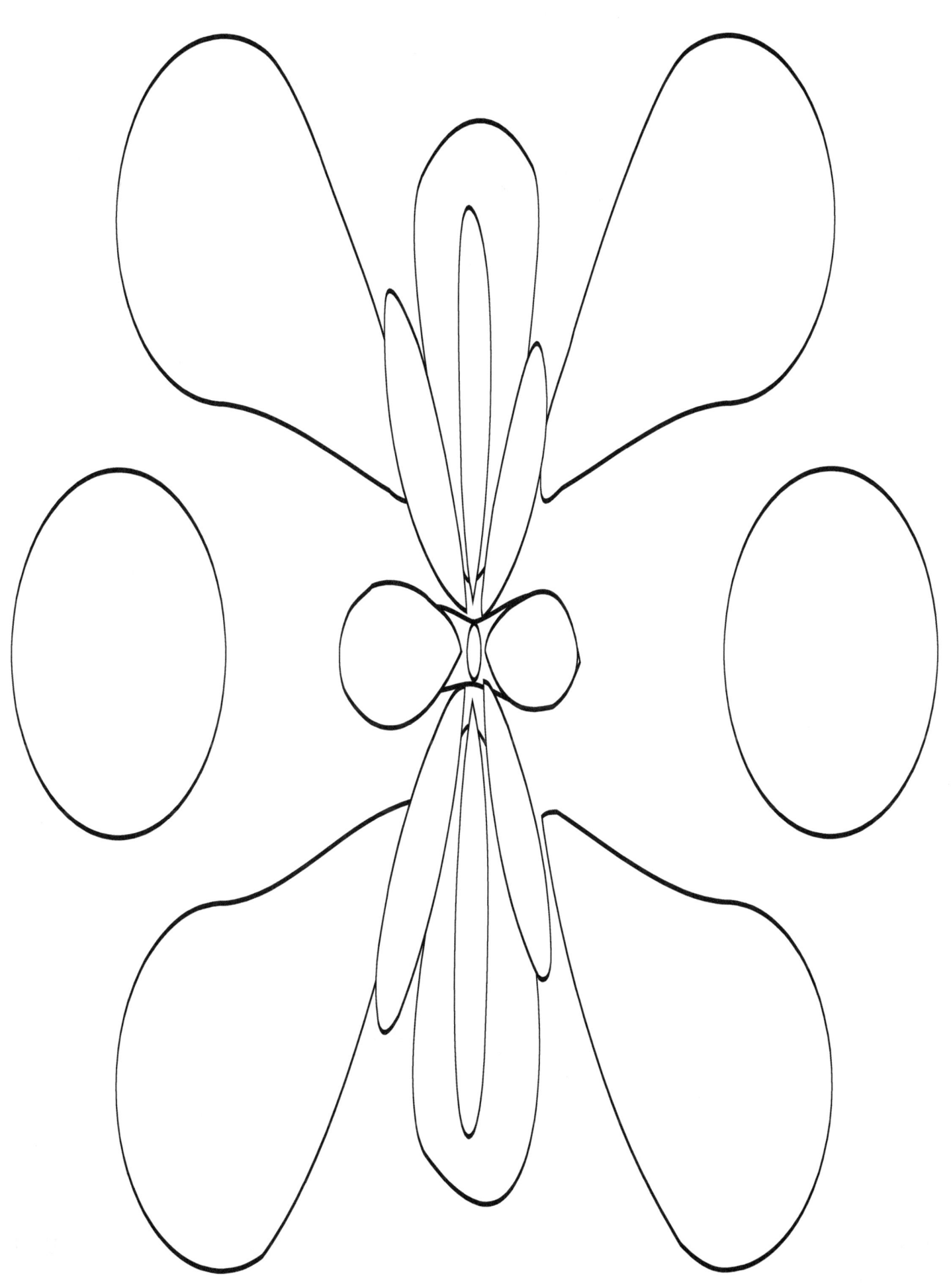

D# 1837

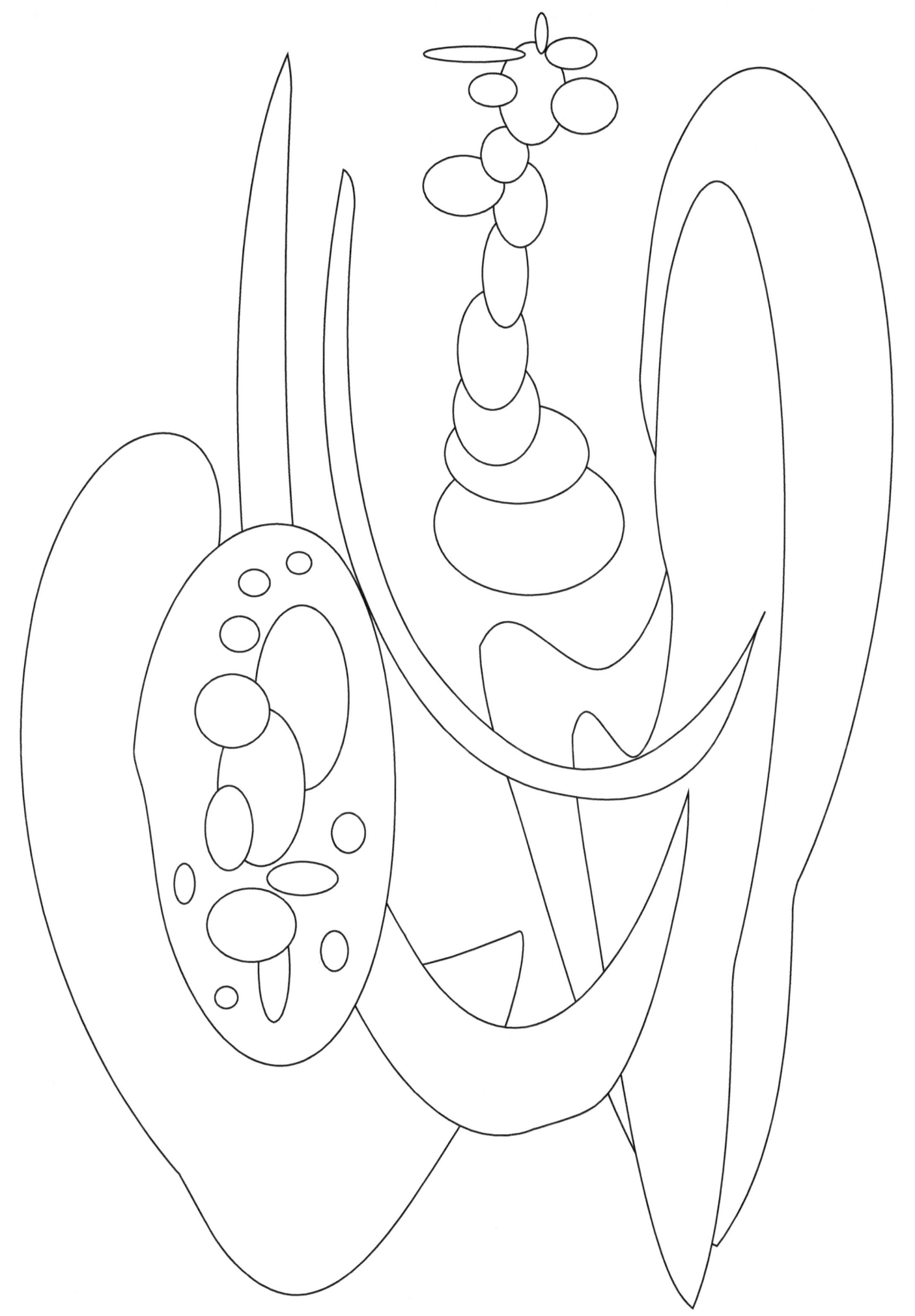

D# 1743

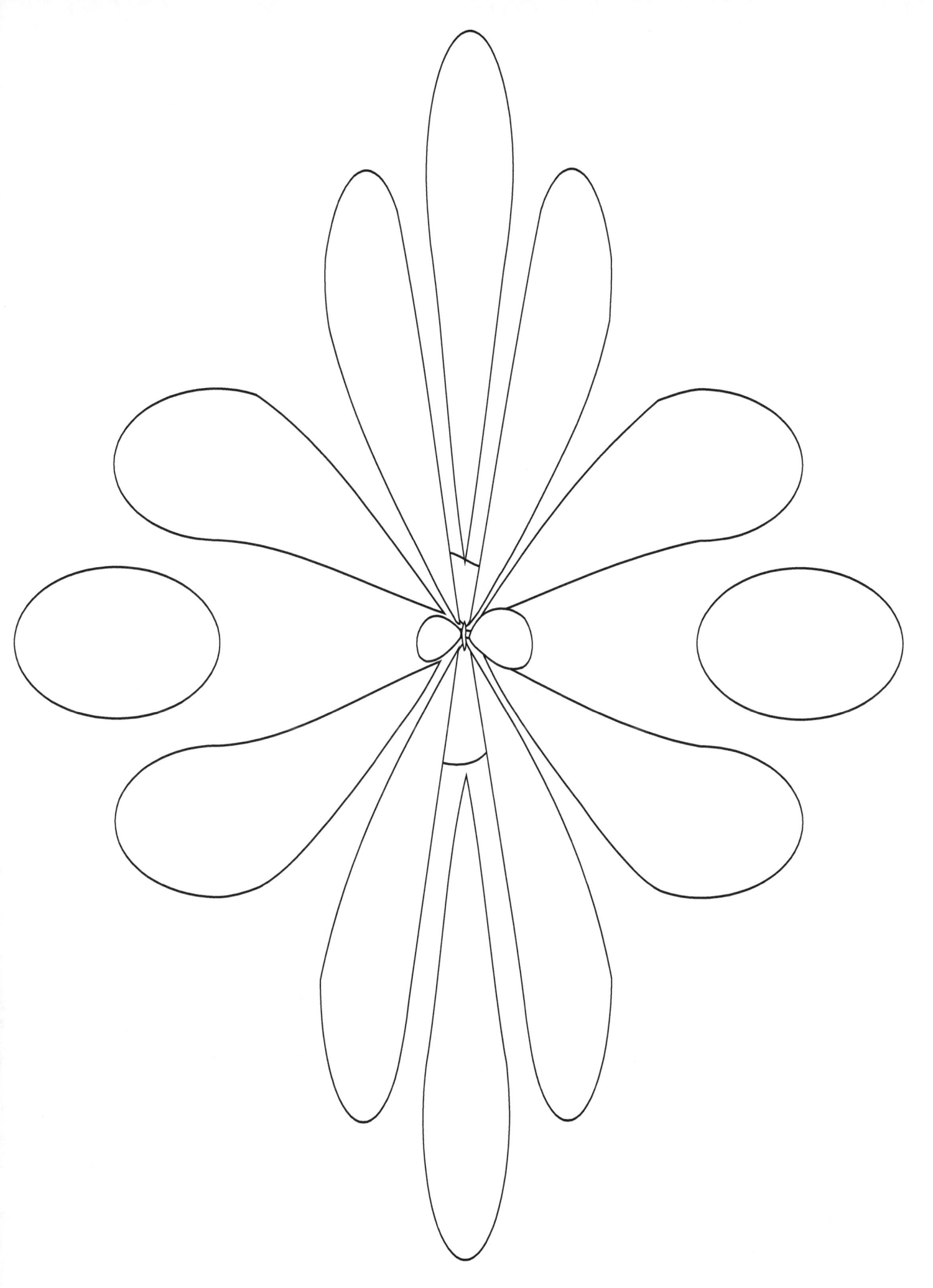